on or before the
...mped...

D1103161

TELEPHONE

French

CHRISTINE BURGESS

CATHERINE ROWLANDS

LONDON SYDNEY AUCKLAND TORONTO

ACKNOWLEDGEMENTS

The authors and publishers would like to thank the following for their help with this book:
Rowan Barnes-Murphy for the illustrations on pages 89 and 109; SNCF for the train ticket on page 55 and the TGV reservation on page 56; Stuart Boreham for the photograph on page 52.

British Library Cataloguing in Publication Data

Burgess, Christine
  Telephone French.
  I. Title   II. Rowlands, Catherine
  448.3

ISBN 0–340–54015–X

First published 1991

© 1991 Christine Burgess and Catherine Rowlands

Typeset by Wearside Tradespools, Fulwell, Sunderland.
Printed in Great Britain for the educational publishing division of Hodder & Stoughton Ltd, Mill Road, Dunton Green, Sevenoaks, Kent by Clays Ltd, St Ives PLC

CONTENTS

Talking business   *Parlons affaires*

INTRODUCTION

Speaking to someone face to face is very different from speaking to someone on the phone. The fact that you can't see the person, their facial expressions or gestures, means that the words and phrases themselves and how you use them become much more important. Telephoning in a foreign language can consequently seem a very daunting task, and it can be a particularly frustrating one if you are trying to cope with a stream of seemingly unintelligible language with possibly long-forgotten, rusty school French.

Our aim, therefore, in writing this book has been twofold: to give you practice in understanding everyday business telephone conversations and to help you find the right words at the right time. Since so much business is conducted on the phone nowadays, we have given all the dialogues a commercial setting, but to avoid lengthy lists of technical vocabulary, we have chosen to concentrate mainly on the food industry. Please note that all company names and all telephone numbers are fictitious.

Telephone French is intended for those of you who already have some background in French. We have designed the course for you to use on your own: the units will help you improve your French, and you can refer to them as the need arises; the two reference sections at the back will help you check words and phrases quickly and easily before or while making a telephone call. The 90-minute cassette, which contains recordings of all the telephone conversations, the key phrases and many of the exercises, is an integral part of the course. The symbol ▣ in the book refers you to the cassette.

For ease of use, each unit follows the same format:

- **Key phrases:** these are the most important phrases and constructions from the dialogues, and appear at the start of each unit both in the book and on the tape. Read them through and listen to them (or the other way around) a few times, and repeat them so that they become familiar. They are in **bold** type in both the English and French texts.

- **Telephone conversations:** all the dialogues are recorded. You may want to try listening to the cassette first without referring to the book at all, or you may want to read through the text first before you listen. Choose whichever approach is right for you. The translations of the dialogues are there, rather like sub-titles in a French film, to help you understand, but you could try following the English as you listen to the French, and you could also try reconstructing the dialogue from the English. The dialogues are annotated, and the numbers draw your attention to footnotes at the bottom of the page, which explain certain points, but which also refer you to pages at the back of the book, i.e. the Grammar Section and Quick Reference section, for fuller explanations and examples. Useful vocabulary is also picked out for you in the English text, and there is a French/English, English/French glossary at the back.

- **Suggested activities:** these offer you further practice on some of the key points that have appeared in the unit. Many of the activities suggest saying things out loud to yourself; this in itself is a valuable exercise, but if you can find a sympathetic partner to practise with, so much the better.

- **Un coup de fil:** in this recorded exercise you are invited to take part in a simulated telephone conversation based on the situation that has been presented in the unit. You will hear the French side of the conversation and a suggested response in English which you have to put into French. A correct version of the French always follows each attempt you make, to allow you to check and, if necessary, correct your response.

- **Reference sections:** the Grammar Section is not a comprehensive review of French grammar, but covers only items which crop up in the dialogues. The Telephone Situations section draws together all the telephone phrases which are used in the dialogues and will help you find any of them again quickly and easily. The same holds true for the Quick Reference sections on the alphabet, numbers, dates and time.

We do realise that some of you will want to dip into individual units as and when they are relevant, as opposed to working through the book progressively. The book is designed to accommodate this, and we hope that the translation will help those of you whose French is more shaky cope with the later units. If you are working through the book progressively, you will find, therefore, that a number of points crop up more than once in the footnotes.

A few words of advice

You will need to be able to understand quite a wide range of vocabulary and structure from native speakers, but you yourself can get by with a much more restricted repertoire of words and phrases. In particular, you do need to be able to ask for something to be repeated and to slow down what is being said to you. It is important not to let the person on the other end say too much at any one time, and it is essential to check each point as it comes, repeating it or asking for it to be repeated if you are unsure. You will find that even a few phrases can help you keep control. Try writing them down, along with one or two of the main points you want to say, before you make the call, just until you feel more confident.

It will take time to build up your skill in handling telephone calls in French, but even ten or fifteen minutes each day spent listening to the dialogues, perhaps in your car, will soon see a big improvement in your ability to understand what is being said to you and in your confidence in knowing what to say in reply.

Finally, it is worth remembering that a few well-rehearsed and well-delivered phrases can make all the difference to how you are received at the other end of the line, and to your subsequent success both on the phone and off it!

Bon courage!

GETTING THROUGH

SPELLING

☎〜〜〜〜〜 KEY PHRASES

Good morning, good afternoon	Bonjour
Hello	Allô
I'd like to speak to . . .	Je voudrais parler à . . .
Could I speak to . . .	Pourrais-je parler à . . .
Who's calling?	C'est de la part de qui?
Who's speaking?	Qui est à l'appareil?
Sarah Johnstone speaking	Sarah Johnstone à l'appareil
Sorry?	Comment?
	Pardon?
Could you repeat that?	Pourriez-vous répéter?
Could you spell your name, please?	Pourriez-vous épeler votre nom, s'il vous plaît?
Just hold on	Ne quittez pas
Wait a moment please	Veuillez patienter
Just a moment	Un instant, s'il vous plaît
I'll put you through (to a man)	Je vous le passe
I'll put you through (to a woman)	Je vous la passe
Speaking (a man)	Lui-même
Speaking (a woman)	Elle-même

DIALOGUE 1

▶ *Hello, Technic France. Good morning.*

▷ *Monsieur Moulin, please.*

▶ *Who's calling?*

▷ *Sarah Johnstone speaking.*

▶ *Right. Hold on, please. I'll put you through.*

▶ **Allô,** Technic France, **bonjour.**

▷ **Monsieur Moulin, s'il vous plaît.**

▶ **C'est de la part de qui?**

▷ **Sarah Johnstone à l'appareil.**

▶ Très bien, Madame. **Ne quittez pas. Je vous le passe.**[1]

1. Pronouns (you, him, me, etc.) come before the verb in French and *vous* always comes before *le* or *la*. See page 118 for examples of the direct and indirect pronouns.

DIALOGUE 2

▶ *EDS, good morning.*

▷ *Yes, hello. I'd like to speak to Madame Simon, please.*

▶ *Who's calling?*

▷ *John Christie.*

▶ *Sorry? Could you repeat that? Mr .. ?*

▷ *Christie.*

▶ *Could you spell your name, please?*

▷ CHRISTIE.

▶ *Thank you. Wait a moment, please. I'll put you through.*

▶ **EDS, bonjour.**

▷ Oui, bonjour. **Je voudrais**[2] **parler** à Madame Simon, s'il vous plaît.

▶ **Qui est à l'appareil?**

▷ John Christie.

▶ **Pardon? Pourriez-vous**[2] **répéter?** Monsieur . . . ?

▷ Christie.

▶ **Pourriez-vous épeler votre nom, s'il vous plaît.**

▷ CHRISTIE.[3]

▶ Merci, Monsieur. **Veuillez patienter. Je vous la passe.**[1]

2. *Je voudrais* (from *vouloir*), *pourrais-je, pourriez-vous* (from *pouvoir*) are in the conditional tense to convey politeness as in English, 'I would like', 'Could I', 'Could you'.

3. There is a guide to help you pronounce the letters of the French alphabet on page 129 as well as the complete telephone alphabet for you to refer to. The alphabet is recorded after the dialogues in this unit.

DIALOGUE 3

▶ *Good morning, Transmanche.*

▷ **Could I speak to** *Monsieur Rocher, please.*

▶ *Yes, who's calling?*

▷ *Andrew Buckingham here.*

▶ *Sorry? Could you spell your name, please?*

▷ BUCKINGHAM.

▶ *B for Berthe or P for Pierre?*

▷ *B for Berthe.*

▶ *Mr Buckingham, yes, and which company are you from?*

▷ *'Pioneer Services' – P for Pierre* IONEER.

▶ *Fine.* **Just a moment, please.** *I'll see if Monsieur Rocher can take the call.*

〰〰〰〰

▶ *Hello? Are you still there? Putting you through to Monsieur Rocher now.*

〰〰〰〰

▶ *Hello, can I help you?*

▷ *Monsieur Rocher?*

▶ *Speaking.*

▶ Transmanche, bonjour.

▷ **Pourrais-je**[1] **parler à** Monsieur Rocher, s'il vous plaît?

▶ Oui, c'est de la part de qui?

▷ Ici Andrew Buckingham.

▶ Comment? Pourriez-vous épeler votre nom, s'il vous plaît?

▷ BUCKINGHAM.[2]

▶ Avec B comme Berthe ou P comme Pierre?

▷ B comme Berthe.

▶ Monsieur Buckingham, oui, et vous êtes de quelle entreprise?

▷ 'Pioneer Services' – P comme Pierre IONEER.

▶ Très bien, Monsieur Buckingham. **Un instant, s'il vous plaît.** Je vais voir si Monsieur Rocher peut prendre la communication.

〰〰〰〰

▶ Allô, vous êtes toujours en ligne? Je vous passe Monsieur Rocher.

〰〰〰〰

▶ Allô, j'écoute.

▷ Monsieur Rocher?

▶ **Lui-même.**

---

to take the call = *prendre la communication*
Are you still there? = *Vous êtes toujours en ligne?*
Hello, can I help you? = *Allô, j'écoute?*

1. See note 2 on page 9.
2. see note 3 on page 9.

SUGGESTED ACTIVITIES

● Listen to the alphabet on the tape and practise saying it all the way through a few times.

● Now listen to the names on the *Liste des Participants* being spelt. Practise spelling them yourself.

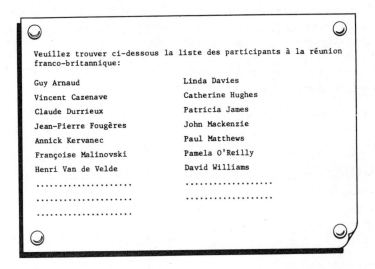

Veuillez trouver ci-dessous la liste des participants à la réunion franco-britannique:

Guy Arnaud	Linda Davies
Vincent Cazenave	Catherine Hughes
Claude Durrieux	Patricia James
Jean-Pierre Fougères	John Mackenzie
Annick Kervanec	Paul Matthews
Françoise Malinovski	Pamela O'Reilly
Henri Van de Velde	David Williams
....	....
....	....
....	

● There are three last minute French participants and one British one whose names do not appear on the list. Listen again to the list and write them in.

● You are the last participant. Add your own name and practise spelling that too.

● Looking at the list of French participants and using *Je voudrais parler à . . .* or *Pourrais-je parler à . . .*, practise asking to speak to each person. Remember to use *Madame* or *Monsieur*, but don't include their first names.

HOW WOULD YOU SAY IN FRENCH?

1 Who's calling, please?
2 Hello, are you still there?
3 Could I speak to Monsieur Mercier?
4 Please hold on.

Coup de fil

In this activity you can take part in a simulated telephone conversation. On the tape you will hear the French side of the conversation followed by a suggested reply in English. There is a short pause at this point to allow you to switch off your cassette recorder and put that reply into French. You will then hear on the tape a correct French version of this reply.

You are Alan or Alison Wright from (*de*) Norscot Textiles and you want to speak to Monsieur Tournier.

UNIT 2

RINGING BACK

TELEPHONE NUMBERS

☎〰〰〰〰 KEY PHRASES

Could you put me through to . . .	Pourriez-vous me passer . . .
The extension is engaged *The line is busy*	Le poste est occupé La ligne est occupée
Do you want to hold? *Would you like to ring back?*	Voulez-vous patienter? Voulez-vous rappeler?
I'll call back later	Je rappellerai plus tard
I'm sorry . . . *I'm sorry . . .*	Je regrette . . . Je suis désolé(e) . . .
Would you repeat that? *Could you repeat that more slowly?*	Voulez-vous répéter? Pourriez-vous répéter plus lentement
I didn't catch the number	Je n'ai pas bien compris le numéro
You've dialled the wrong number *I'm sorry to have troubled you*	Vous avez fait un faux numéro Je vous prie de m'excuser

DIALOGUE 1

▷ *Monsieur Masson, please.*

▷ Monsieur Masson, s'il vous plaît.

▶ **I'm sorry, the line's busy. Do you want to hold?**

▶ **Je suis désolée, Madame, la ligne est occupée. Voulez-vous[1] patienter?**

▷ *No. **I'll call back later.***

▷ Non, non. **Je rappellerai[2] plus tard.**

DIALOGUE 2

▶ *Good afternoon, Europ Service.*

▶ Bonjour, Europ Service.

▷ *Could you put me through to Madame Richard, please.*

▷ **Pourriez-vous me passer** Madame Richard, s'il vous plaît.

▶ *I'm sorry, her extension's engaged. Would you like to ring back?*

▶ **Je suis désolée, Monsieur, le poste est occupé. Voulez-vous rappeler?**

▷ *I'll ring her back this afternoon. What's her extension number?*

▷ Je la rappellerai cet après-midi. Quel est son numéro de poste?

▶ *Extension 3648. But she'll be at our Neuilly office this afternoon. Do you want me to give you the number?*

▶ Poste 3648. Ah, mais cet après-midi elle sera[2] à notre bureau de Neuilly. Voulez-vous que[1] je vous donne le numéro?

---

her extension number = *son numéro de poste*

1. *Voulez-vous* + infinitive, e.g. **Voulez-vous** *patienter* means 'do you want to hold'.
Voulez-vous que je . . ., e.g. **Voulez-vous que je vous donne . . .** means 'do you want me to give you . . .'. The verb after *voulez-vous que* is in the subjunctive form (see page 120), though it is not different from the indicative in this example.

2. This is the future tense: 'I will ring back'. See page 115 for the future tense endings. Note also *je serai*: 'I will be', *il/elle sera*: 'she will be'. See page 116 for irregular verbs.

▷ *Yes, please*

▶ *Wait a moment. It's 45 08 76 92.*

▷ **Could you repeat** *the number* **more slowly,** *please.*

▶ *45 08 76 92*

▷ *Sorry.* **Would you repeat** *the last number.*

▶ *92*

▷ *Thank you. Goodbye.*

▷ Oui, s'il vous plaît.

▶ Attendez . . . C'est le 45 08 76 92.[1]

▷ **Pourriez-vous répéter** le numéro **plus lentement,** s'il vous plaît.

▶ Le 45 08 76 92.

▷ Pardon, Mademoiselle, **voulez-vous**[2] **répéter** le dernier chiffre?

▶ 92.

▷ Merci, Mademoiselle, au revoir.

---

wait a moment = *attendez*
the last number = *le dernier chiffre*

1. All telephone numbers in France now have eight digits, the first two being the regional code.
In Belgium and Switzerland 70 is *septante* and 90 is *nonante*. The Belgians use *octante* for 80, but the Swiss use *huitante*. See page 130 for the list of numbers.

2. *Voulez-vous* here means 'Would you' when asking someone to do something.

DIALOGUE   3

▶ *Hello, can I help you?*

▷ *Monsieur Lefèvre, please.*

▶ *Monsieur Lefèvre. Do you know his extension number?*

▷ *No, but he's the sales manager.*

▶ *I'm afraid* **you've dialled the wrong number.** *This is 78 28 09 64.*

▶ Allô, j'écoute.

▷ Monsieur Lefèvre, s'il vous plaît.

▶ Monsieur Lefèvre? Est-ce que[1] vous connaissez son numéro de poste?

▷ Non, mais il est directeur des ventes.

▶ Ah non, **vous avez fait un faux numéro.** Ici c'est le 78 28 09 64.

---

the sales manager = *le directeur des ventes*

▷ Yes, so I have. **I'm sorry to have troubled you.**

〰〰〰〰

► Good morning. Delmas et fils.

▷ Monsieur Lefèvre, please.

► I'm sorry but Monsieur Lefèvre is away on business today. Do you want him to ring you back?

▷ Yes, please.

► You are Mr . . .?

▷ Darbyshire, Peter Darbyshire.

► How do you spell that?

▷ Sorry?

► Could you spell your surname.

▷ DARBYSHIRE.

► And which company are you from?

▷ Webb & Co. in London.

► What's your telephone number?

▷ 255 6387.

► Sorry, **I didn't catch the number.**

▷ 255 6387 and the code for London is 71.

► Right. Monsieur Lefèvre will ring you back tomorrow.

▷ Ah, en effet. **Je vous prie de m'excuser.**

〰〰〰〰

► Allô, Delmas et fils, bonjour.

▷ Monsieur Lefèvre, s'il vous plaît.

► Je regrette mais Monsieur Lefèvre est en déplacement aujourd'hui. Vous voulez[1] qu'il vous rappelle?

▷ Oui, s'il vous plaît.

► Vous êtes Monsieur . . . ?

▷ Darbyshire, Peter Darbyshire.

► Cela s'écrit comment, Monsieur?

▷ Pardon, Madame?

► Pourriez-vous[1] épeler votre nom de famille?

▷ DARBYSHIRE.

► Et vous êtes de quelle société?

▷ Webb & Co. à Londres.

► Quel est votre numéro de téléphone?

▷ 255 63 87.

► Pardon, **je n'ai pas bien compris le numéro,** Monsieur.

▷ 255 63 87 et l'indicatif pour Londres est le 71.

► Très bien, Monsieur. Monsieur Lefèvre vous rappellera[2] demain.

---

away on business = en déplacement
company = la société
the code = l'indicatif

1. The three ways of forming questions are shown on page 113.

2. See note on the future on page 14.

▷ *Tomorrow morning, if possible. I'll only be here until midday.*

▷ Demain matin, si c'est possible. Je serai ici jusqu'à midi seulement.

▶ *OK then. Bye.*

▶ Oui, au revoir, Monsieur.

only = *seulement*
until midday = *jusqu'à midi*

SUGGESTED ACTIVITIES

🔘 • Listen to the numbers being read out on the tape. You'll hear from 1 to 31, then 40, 50, 60 and then 70 to 99. Use the list on page 130 if you would like to see them written down. Now go over them again a few times, practising them out loud.

• Work out how you would say the telephone numbers on the publicity sheet.

Biscuits Délices

C'est déjà l'Europe de la gourmandise.

Siège social : 151 Place de la Paix 75018 Paris

☎ (1) 42.13.59.92   Fax (1) 42.13.60.60   Télex 81562 F

AGENCES EN FRANCE:
• Marseille 91.37.89.15
• Lyon   74.26.44.04
• Bordeaux   56.39.67.98
• Rennes   99.62.06.16

SUCCURSALES EN GRANDE BRETAGNE:
• Londres   (081) 807 2277
• Edimbourg (031) 552 3488
• Cardiff   (0222) 670419
• Belfast   (0232) 590669

BUREAU EN BELGIQUE:
• Bruxelles (2) 648.31.33

BUREAU EN SUISSE:
• Genève (22) 44.77.00

🔘 • Follow these numbers on the tape now. There is one printing mistake and one of the numbers has since been changed. See if you can spot them.

• *Le numéro de notre bureau à Neuilly est le 45 08 76 92.* Follow this example and go through the list of offices and telephone numbers again, changing the information as appropriate, e.g. *Le numéro de notre bureau à Rennes est le 99 62 06 16,* etc.

• Make sure you can give your own office number in French before you leave this unit. Divide the number up as follows:

733 573 48 (if it has 5 digits)
532 68 56 90 (if it has 6 digits)

☎〰〰〰〰 HOW WOULD YOU SAY IN FRENCH?

1 I'll call back this afternoon.
2 He'll be here until midday.
3 She can ring you back tomorrow morning.
4 It's the wrong number.

Coup de fil

You are trying to ring Monsieur Thomas, but you find you have to note down the number and ring him back.

LEAVING A MESSAGE

TIME

 **KEY PHRASES**

Do you want to leave a message?	Voulez-vous laisser un message?
Can I take a message?	Je peux prendre un message?
Could you take a message?	Pourriez-vous prendre un message?
I'll give him/her the message	Je lui ferai la commission
Tell him/her that . . .	Dites-lui que . . .
Ask him/her to . . .	Demandez-lui de . . .
When will she be back?	Quand sera-t-elle de retour?
She will be back . . .	Elle sera de retour . . .
Sorry? I didn't quite catch that	Pardon? Je n'ai pas bien compris
Just a moment, I'll write that down	Attendez, je note
What time is it?	Quelle heure est-il?
I see	Ah bon
The line's bad	La ligne est mauvaise
Could you speak up a bit, please?	Pourriez-vous parler un peu plus fort, s'il vous plaît?

DIALOGUE 1

▶ *Hello, can I help you.*

▷ *I'd like to speak to Monsieur Durand, please. Paul Whyte here.*

▶ *I'm sorry. Monsieur Durand isn't here today.* **Would you like to leave a message?**

▷ *Yes. Tell Monsieur Durand that I'll ring back tomorrow around 11.*

▶ Allô, j'écoute.

▷ J'aimerais parler à Monsieur Durand, s'il vous plaît. Paul Whyte à l'appareil.

▶ Je suis désolée. Monsieur Durand n'est pas là aujourd'hui. **Voulez-vous laisser un message?**

▷ Oui. Dites à Monsieur Durand que je rappellerai demain vers 11 heures.

---

around = *vers*

DIALOGUE 2

▷ *Could you put me through to Monsieur Legrand, please.*

▶ *I'm sorry but Monsieur Legrand has a meeting this morning from 9 till 11.30. Can I give him a message?*

▷ **Sorry? I didn't quite catch that.**

▶ **Can I take a message?**

▷ *Oh, a message! Yes, please.*

▶ *You are Mr . . . ?*

▷ *David Taylor from Burtex in Liverpool.*

▷ Pourriez-vous me passer Monsieur Legrand, s'il vous plaît.

▶ Je suis navrée mais Monsieur Legrand est en réunion ce matin de 9h à 11h30. Je peux lui faire une commission?

▷ **Pardon? Je n'ai pas bien compris,** Madame.

▶ **Je peux prendre un message?**[1]

▷ Ah, un message! Oui, s'il vous plaît.

▶ Vous êtes Monsieur . . . ?

▷ David Taylor de Burtex à Liverpool.

---

sorry = *navré(e)*
at a meeting = *en réunion*
to give someone a message = *faire une commission*

1. Another example of a question indicated by raising the voice.

▶ *And can you tell me what it's about?*

▷ *It's in connection with the conference. Monsieur Legrand knows all about it.* **Tell him that** *I'll ring him back this afternoon.*

▶ *Fine.* **I'll give him the message** *but he won't be back before 3.30.*

▷ *OK. I'll ring him after 3.30. Thank you. Bye.*

▶ Oui, et c'est à quel sujet?

▷ Au sujet de la conférence. Monsieur Legrand est au courant. **Dites-lui**[1] **que** je le rappellerai cet après-midi.

▶ Très bien, Monsieur, **je lui ferai**[2] **la commission** mais il ne sera pas de retour avant 15h30.

▷ D'accord. Je le rappellerai après 15h30. Merci, Madame, au revoir.

What's it about? = *C'est à quel sujet?*
in connection with/about = *au sujet de*
he knows = *il est au courant*

1. *Dites à **Monsieur Durand** → Dites-lui* (Tell him)
*Demandez à **Madame Thomas*** *→ Demandez-lui* (Ask her)
Usually the indirect pronoun (*lui* = (to) him/her) would come before the verb but here it comes after because the verb is in the imperative form.

2. *Je **lui** ferai, je **lui** parle, je **lui** dirai*: three examples of *lui* coming before the verb. See page 118 for more examples of the word order. *Faire, dire, être* are in the future tense. See page 116.

DIALOGUE 3

▷ *Could I speak to Madame Thomas, please. Bill Watt speaking.*

▶ *I'm sorry, Madame Thomas has gone on a course today.*

▷ *The line is very bad. Could you speak up a bit, please?*

▶ *Madame Thomas isn't here. She's on a course all day.*

▷ Pourrais-je parler à Madame Thomas, s'il vous plaît? Bill Watt à l'appareil.

▶ Je suis désolée mais Madame Thomas suit un stage aujourd'hui.

▷ **La ligne est mauvaise. Pourriez-vous parler un peu plus fort, s'il vous plaît?**

▶ Madame Thomas est absente. Elle est en stage toute la journée.

---

to go on a training course = *suivre un stage*
all day = *toute la journée*

▷ **When will she be back?** I must speak to her today.

▷ **Quand sera-t-elle de retour?** Il faut que je lui parle[1] aujourd'hui-même.

▶ I don't know exactly but let's say around 5.

▶ Je ne sais pas exactement, Monsieur. Disons vers 17 heures.

▷ **I see. Could you take a message** please? It is very important that I speak to her.

▷ **Ah bon. Pourriez-vous prendre un message,** s'il vous plaît? Il est très important que je lui parle.[1]

▶ Yes, of course.

▶ Mais certainement.

▷ **Ask her to ring me back** this evening after 6.30. I'll give you my home number. It's 367 2972.

▷ **Demandez-lui[2] de** me rappeler ce soir après 18h30. Je vous donne mon numéro personnel. C'est le 367 29 72.

▶ **Just a moment, I'll write that down.** 367 2912.

▶ **Attendez, je note.** 367 29 12.

▷ No, not 12, 72.

▷ Non, non. Pas 12, 72.

▶ And what's the code?

▶ Précédé de quel indicatif?

▷ 81 for London.

▷ 81 pour Londres.

▶ Fine. I'll tell her as soon as **she gets back.**

▶ Très bien. Je le lui dirai[3] dès qu'**elle sera de retour.**

▷ Tell me, **what time is it** in France at the moment.

▷ Dites-moi, **quelle heure est-il** en France actuellement?

---

my home number = *mon numéro personnel*
as soon as = *dès que*
at the moment = *actuellement*

1. *Il faut que* ... This is a phrase you will find used quite frequently in these conversations. Literally it means 'it is necessary that ...', but it is more normally translated as 'I have to/you have to ...'. Though not obvious here, the verb form after *il faut que* and *il est très important que* is the subjunctive. See page 120.

2. See note 2 on page 21.

3. See note 3 on page 21.

▶ 2.40.

▷ *I see. In that case ask Madame Thomas to call me back after 7.30, French time.*

▶ *I will do. Goodbye.*

▶ 14h40.[1]

▷ **Ah bon.** Alors, dans ce cas demandez à Madame Thomas de me rappeler après 19h30, heure française.[2]

▶ Très bien, Monsieur, au revoir.

---

in that case = *dans ce cas*

1. In a business context, whether you are arranging meetings or simply giving the time of day, you should use the 24 hour clock (see page 132). This is normal practice in Europe and avoids any confusion.

2. Remember that Britain is an hour behind the other EEC countries for most of the year.

SUGGESTED ACTIVITIES

• Listen to the times from the 24-hour clock that are recorded on the tape. You'll find them on page 132.

• Take a particular hour, 14h for example, and practise going round a whole hour, every five minutes.

• How would you say: 13h30, 14h45, 16h15, 17h40, 19h55, 21h25?

• Look at the grid below, and go through the different sections revising spelling and telephone numbers.

Bob Ross	PMB	0272 540212	aujourd'hui avant 15h	la réunion
Daniel Allegret	Forum-Info	61 61 97 10	demain après 14h	sa lettre
Rosemary Davidson	SEMCO	0782 315578	cet après-midi vers 16h	son télex
Catherine Pinelli	Euromed	88 65 01 56	ce soir à 20h30	l'exposition
Jim Evans	Scotexport	041 634 3995	plus tard	le contrat

• Practise leaving a message with a secretary or colleague to ask Monsieur Coupaud to ring you back.

e.g. *Bob Ross de PMB à l'appareil. Mon numéro de téléphone est le 272 54 02 12. Demandez à Monsieur Coupaud (or demandez-lui) de me rappeler avant 15h. C'est au sujet de la réunion.*

Remember: *au sujet de la, au sujet de l'. . .,* but *au sujet du.*

🕿〰〰〰〰 **HOW WOULD YOU SAY IN FRENCH?**

1 She'll be back around 3 o'clock.
2 He has a meeting all day.
3 Could you take a message.
4 Ask her to phone me back after 4 o'clock.

Coup de fil

You're Michèle or Michael Foster and you're trying to contact Monsieur Aubert who is at a meeting all day and who won't be in the office tomorrow either. You leave a message.

MAKING AN APPOINTMENT

DAYS AND DATES

☎〰〰〰〰 KEY PHRASES

Can I help you?	Puis-je vous renseigner?
I'd like to meet . . .	Je voudrais rencontrer . . .
I'd like to make an appointment	Je voudrais prendre rendez-vous
I have nothing planned	Je n'ai rien de prévu
I'm very busy	Je suis très pris(e)
She could see you at 2.15	Elle pourrait vous recevoir à 14h15
I can offer you 10.30	Je peux vous proposer 10h30
That's OK	Ça tombe bien
That's not very suitable	Ça tombe mal
That suits me perfectly	Ça me convient très bien
That doesn't suit me	Ça ne me convient pas
That's fine	C'est parfait
That's a bit difficult	Ça me paraît difficile

DIALOGUE 1

▶ *Monsieur Chapin's secretary, good morning.*

▶ Secrétariat de Monsieur Chapin, bonjour.

▷ *Good morning, Alison Goodwin speaking.* **I'd like to make an appointment** *with Monsieur Chapin this week, if that's possible.*

▷ Bonjour, Alison Goodwin à l'appareil. **Je voudrais prendre rendez-vous** avec Monsieur Chapin cette semaine, si c'est possible.

▶ *Yes . . . Wednesday?*

▶ Oui, Madame. . . . Mercredi?

▷ **That's OK.** *At what time?*

▷ Oui, **ça tombe bien.** A quelle heure?

▶ *Let's see . . . at 11.15?*

▶ Voyons . . . à 11h15?

▷ *Yes,* **that's fine.**

▷ Oui, **c'est parfait.**

▶ *Right. That's Wednesday the 19th at 11.15.*

▶ Très bien, Madame, mercredi 19 à 11h15.

let's see . . . = *voyons . . .*

DIALOGUE 2

▷ *Madame Delmas, please.*

▷ Madame Delmas, s'il vous plaît.

▶ *Madame Delmas is in Portugal on holiday at the moment, and she won't be back before the end of the week.* **Can I help you?** *I'm her secretary.*

▶ Madame Delmas est actuellement en congé[1] au Portugal et elle ne sera pas de retour avant la fin de la semaine. **Puis-je[2] vous renseigner?** Je suis sa secrétaire.

▷ *Yes, I'm sure you can.* **I'd like to meet** *Madame Delmas as soon as possible.*

▷ Oui, certainement. **Je voudrais rencontrer** Madame Delmas le plus tôt possible.

on holiday = *en congé*
the end of the week = *la fin de la semaine*
as soon as possible = *le plus tôt possible*

1. The French tend to take four weeks' holiday either in July or August.

2. *Je peux → puis-je* when the two words are reversed at the start of a sentence.

▶ *OK. Just a moment. I'll check her diary. **She's already very busy** all day Monday. Tuesday . . . em, no, Tuesday's not possible either and then on Wednesday she has to go to Lyon. But **she doesn't have anything arranged** for either Thursday or Friday.*

▷ *I'd prefer Thursday. I have to be in Lyon myself on Friday.*

▶ *Morning or afternoon? **I can offer you** 10 o'clock or 11.30. Ah, no, sorry, not the morning. **She could see you** at 2.15.*

▷ *Yes, **that suits me perfectly.***

▶ *Well, I'll just take a note of that . . . Thursday 30th August at 2.15. And you are Mr . . . ?*

▷ *King, KING, Charles King.*

▶ *Right then, Mr King. Goodbye.*

▶ D'accord. Attendez, je vérifie sur son agenda. Lundi **elle est déjà très prise** toute la journée. Euh, mardi . . . ah, non, mardi ce n'est pas possible[1] non plus, et puis mercredi il faut qu'elle aille[2] à Lyon. Mais **elle n'a rien[1] de prévu** ni jeudi ni vendredi.

▷ Je préfèrerais jeudi. Il faut que je sois[2] moi aussi à Lyon vendredi.

▶ Le matin ou l'après-midi? . . . **Je peux vous proposer** 10 heures ou 11h30. Ah non, pardon, pas le matin. Euh, **elle pourrait vous recevoir** à 14h15.

▷ Oui, **ça me convient très bien.**

▶ Alors, je note . . . jeudi, 30 août[3] à 14h15. Et vous êtes Monsieur . . . ?

▷ King, KING, Charles King.

▶ Très bien, Monsieur King. Au revoir.

to check her diary = *vérifier sur son agenda*
in the morning = *le matin*
in the afternoon = *l'après-midi*

1. See page 113 for those phrases which use *ne*.

2. You will notice the subjunctive form of the verb in these examples. *Etre* and *aller* have irregular forms. See page 120.

3. The days of the week and months of the year are listed on page 131.

DIALOGUE 3

▷ Monsieur Sylvestre, please.

▷ Monsieur Sylvestre, s'il vous plaît.

▶ I'm sorry, Monsieur Sylvestre doesn't work here any more but I'll put you through to Monsieur Dubarry who's taken over from him. If you could just wait a moment.

▶ Je regrette, Monsieur Sylvestre ne travaille plus[1] ici mais je vais vous passer son remplaçant, Monsieur Dubarry. Veuillez patienter quelques instants.

〰〰〰

▶ Monsieur Dubarry's secretary.

〰〰〰

▶ Secrétariat de Monsieur Dubarry.

▷ Good afternoon, John Gordon from Glendale Ltd. in Scotland here. I'd like to speak to Monsieur Dubarry.

▷ Bonjour. Ici John Gordon de Glendale Ltd. en Ecosse. J'aimerais parler à Monsieur Dubarry.

▶ I'm sorry, Mr Gordon. Monsieur Dubarry is in the States on business.

▶ Je suis désolée, Monsieur Gordon. Monsieur Dubarry est en voyage d'affaires aux Etats-Unis.[2]

▷ I see. I'm planning to come to France for the Trade Fair from the 14th to the 24th and **I'd like to meet** Monsieur Dubarry either next week or the week after.

▷ Ah bon. J'ai l'intention de venir en France pour la Foire Exposition du 14 au 24 et **je voudrais rencontrer** Monsieur Dubarry soit la semaine prochaine soit la semaine suivante.

▶ Yes, I understand, but Monsieur Dubarry doesn't get back until the 13th.

▶ Oui, je comprends mais Monsieur Dubarry ne revient que[1] le 13 mai.

▷ **I've nothing arranged** for Thursday the 15th.

▷ **Je n'ai rien de prévu** le jeudi 15.

---

on a business trip = *en voyage d'affaires*
I'm planning to = *J'ai l'intention de*
the Trade Fair = *la Foire Exposition*
next week = *la semaine prochaine*
the following week = *la semaine suivante*
either . . . or = *soit . . . soit*

1. See page 113 for those phrases which use *ne* and their different meanings.

2. All feminine countries, e.g. *la France, la Belgique, l'Angleterre* take *en* meaning 'to' or 'in'. Masculine countries such as *le Japon, le Canada, le Portugal* take *au*. Note the plural *aux Etats-Unis*.

▶ *Oh dear, no! That's a public holiday. It's Ascension Day. We never work then.*

▶ Oh là là! Non, c'est un jour férié. C'est la fête de l'Ascension.[1] Nous ne travaillons jamais[2] ce jour-là.

▷ *Friday . . . ?*

▷ Vendredi . . . ?

▶ *That's not possible either. We'll be making a long weekend of it.*

▶ Ce n'est pas possible non plus.[1] Nous faisons le pont.

▷ *Sorry? I don't understand that at all.*

▷ Comment? Je ne comprends pas du tout.

▶ *We're not working on Friday either since there's only one day between the public holiday and the weekend. We're having a long weekend. But just a moment . . . he'll be in the office all day Monday.*

▶ Nous ne travaillons pas vendredi non plus parce qu'il n'y a qu'un seul jour entre le jour férié et le weekend. Nous faisons le pont. Mais attendez . . . lundi il sera au bureau toute la journée.

▷ *No, **Monday's a bit difficult.** I have to be at the Fair all day – I already have several appointments. Could Monsieur Dubarry see me on Tuesday in the afternoon?*

▷ Non, **lundi me paraît difficile.** Il faut que je sois[3] à la Foire toute la journée. J'ai déjà plusieurs rendez-vous. Est-ce que Monsieur Dubarry pourrait me recevoir mardi dans l'après-midi?

▶ *Yes, at 3.45.*

▶ Oui, à 15h45?

▷ *Yes, **that's fine.***

▷ Oui, **c'est parfait.**

▶ *Right, I'll make a note of that . . . Tuesday 20th May at 3.45 in our office.*

▶ Bien, je note . . . mardi 20 mai à 15h45 dans nos bureaux.

▷ *Good. I'll ring from Paris to confirm our appointment.*

▷ Très bien, Madame. Je téléphonerai de Paris pour[4] confirmer notre rendez-vous.

▶ *Right then. Bye.*

▶ Très bien, Monsieur. Au revoir.

---

a public holiday = *un jour férié*
several = *plusieurs*

1. See page 132 for a list of the public holidays in France, Belgium and Switzerland.
2. See note 1 on page 28.
3. See note 2 on page 27.
4. *pour* followed by an infinitive means 'in order to . . .'.

☎〰〰〰〰 SUGGESTED ACTIVITIES

🔘 • Listen to the days of the week and months of the year on the tape and practise repeating them.

• Some dates have been ringed in the section from the calendar below. Practise saying firstly the dates, and then the days and dates out loud, e.g. *le 5 juin, mercredi 5 juin*.

Juillet							Août						
L	M	M	J	V	S	D		L	M	M	J	V	S	D
①	2	3	4	5	6	7					1	②	3	4
8	9	10	11	12	13	⑭		5	6	7	8	9	⑩	11
15	16	17	18	19	20	21		12	13	14	⑮	16	17	18
22	㉓	24	25	26	27	28		19	20	㉑	22	23	24	25
29	30	㉛						26	27	28	29	30	31	

• You are trying to make an appointment with Monsieur Liard, an extract from whose diary appears opposite. How would you suggest the following days and times?

Monday, 29th October at 11 am.
Tuesday, 30th October at 12 o'clock.
Wednesday, 31st October at 9.30 am.
Thursday, 1st November at 3.15 pm.

• Imagine his replies to each of your suggestions.

• Looking at his diary, what possibilities could he offer you? e.g. *Je peux vous proposer . . .*

☎〰〰〰〰 HOW WOULD YOU SAY IN FRENCH?

1 She can't see you at 12 o'clock.
2 I'm very busy all day.
3 He only gets back on Wednesday 21st August.
4 I'd like to have an appointment with her before the end of the week.

LUNDI **29**	MARDI **30**	MERCREDI **31**	JEUDI **1**	VENDREDI **2**
s Narcisse Tx 302	s Bienvenue Tx 303	s Quentin Tx 304	Toussaint Tx 305	Défunts Tx 306

8 Départ 7h 50
Orly
9 Arrivée
Toulouse
10 8h 55

10h16 Roissy
vol BA 184
M. Duke

} Réunion

FERIÉ

11 } M. Fournier
12 61.30.40.51

} déjeuner
d'affaires

} Visite
Usine

⑮ Mme
leclerc

} Visite
Atelier
production

18h02
gare ST
lazare

normandie

normandie

19 Retour
Paris.
20 vol
Ai 595
21 19h10

Impératif	Impératif	Impératif	Impératif	Impératif

Coup de fil

You are Claire or Charles Murray and you are trying to arrange an
appointment with Madame Leguet.

UNIT 5

CONFIRMING AN APPOINTMENT

DIRECTIONS

☎〰〰〰 KEY PHRASES

Our meeting is at 10.30, isn't it?	Nous avons bien rendez-vous à 10h30, n'est-ce pas?
I'm ringing to confirm our meeting	Je vous appelle pour confirmer notre rendez-vous
Could you tell me how to get to your office? *Do you know how to get to . . . ?*	Pourriez-vous m'indiquer comment me rendre à vos bureaux? Vous savez vous rendre à . . . ?
It would be better to take the RER	Il vaut mieux prendre le RER
You have to take the exit B	Il faut prendre la sortie B
You have to change	Il faut que vous changiez
Just a moment, let me repeat that *I'll have to write all that down*	Attendez, je répète Il faut que je note tout ça
Is it easy to park nearby?	On peut se garer facilement dans le quartier?
See you later *See you in a little while*	A plus tard A tout à l'heure

DIALOGUE 1

▷ *Monsieur Dulac, please.*

▷ Monsieur Dulac, s'il vous plaît.

▶ *Speaking.*

▶ Lui-même.

▷ *Good morning, Monsieur Dulac. John Powell speaking. I've just arrived at Charles de Gaulle airport. Our meeting is at 10.30, isn't it?*

▷ Bonjour, Monsieur Dulac. John Powell à l'appareil. Je viens d'arriver[1] à l'aéroport Charles de Gaulle. **Nous avons bien rendez-vous à 10h30, n'est-ce pas?**

▶ *Yes, that's right. Do you know how to get to our head office?*

▶ Oui, c'est cela. **Vous savez vous rendre[2]** au siège de notre compagnie?

▷ *No, it's the first time I've been to la Défense.*

▷ Non, c'est la première fois que je viens à la Défense.[3]

▶ *In that case, take a taxi. That's the easiest thing to do. What time is it now? 9.05. Um, with the traffic jams, you'll never make it on time. It would be better to take the RER.*

▶ Dans ce cas, prenez[4] un taxi. C'est le plus facile. Quelle heure est-il? 9h05. Ah, oui, mais avec les embouteillages, vous ne serez jamais à l'heure! **Il vaut mieux prendre le RER.**[5]

▷ *The RER to . . . ?*

▷ Le RER jusqu'à . . .

---

head office = *le siège*
traffic jam = *l'embouteillage*
on time = *à l'heure*

1. *venir de* + infinitive = to have just . . .
e.g. *Je viens d'arriver* = I've just arrived
Nous venons de le recevoir = We've just received it.

2. *se rendre* = to go, get oneself to. See page 119 for the pattern of these reflexive verbs.

3. An important new business centre on the outskirts of Paris.

4. *Prenez* without *vous* is the form of the verb used, as here, to give instructions. See also *descendez*: 'get off' and *demandez*: 'ask'.

5. New and fast rail network linking suburbs and city centre.

▶ Yes, take the RER at Roissy straight through to Châtelet-les-Halles. **You have to change** there. Then get on the train going to St Germain-en-Laye. Get off at la Défense and **you have to leave** by the exit marked Esplanade B. The Tour Europe is five minutes' walk from there.

▷ **Just a moment, I'll go through that again.** Right, at the airport I take the RER. I change at Châtelet, and I take a second train to . . .

▶ St Germain.

▷ OK. And at la Défense I take exit B.

▶ Yes, Esplanade B. It's the nearest one to our office.

▷ Right.

▶ When you arrive, go to reception on the ground floor and ask the receptionist to contact me.

▷ Great. **I'll see you later** then.

▶ Yes. **I'll see you in a little while.**

▶ Oui, prenez le RER à Roissy. C'est direct jusqu'à Châtelet-les-Halles. Là **il faut que vous changiez.**[1] Prenez la correspondance en direction de St Germain-en-Laye. Descendez[2] à la Défense. **Il faut prendre**[3] la sortie Esplanade B. La Tour Europe est à cinq minutes à pied.

▷ **Attendez, je répète.** Donc, à l'aéroport je prends le RER. Je change à Châtelet et je prends un deuxième RER pour . . .

▶ Direction St Germain.

▷ D'accord. A la Défense, c'est la sortie B.

▶ Oui, Esplanade B. C'est la plus près de nos bureaux.

▷ Très bien.

▶ Lorsque vous arrivez, adressez-vous[4] au bureau d'accueil au rez-de-chaussée et demandez[2] à la réceptionniste de me contacter.

▷ Parfait. **A plus tard.**[5]

▶ **A tout à l'heure.**[5]

---

the connection = la correspondance
exit = la sortie
reception = le bureau d'accueil
the ground floor = le rez-de-chaussée

1. Il faut que . . . followed by the subjunctive.

2. See note 4 on page 33.

3. Il faut + infinitive is a more general instruction. Notice the similar il vaut mieux prendre 'it would be better to take'.

4. See note 2 on page 33.

5. What to say when you are due to see the person in the not too distant future; e.g. also à demain, à jeudi, à la semaine prochaine.

DIALOGUE 2

▶ Hotel reception, can I help you?

▷ Room 225. I'd like to make an outside call.

▶ Certainly.

▷ The number is 47 63 28 16.

▶ Hold on please. I'll get it for you.

〰〰〰〰

▶ Mr Brown, you're through.

〰〰〰〰

▶ Hello?

▷ Good morning. Roger Brown speaking. **I'm ringing to confirm my appointment** with Monsieur Sellier.

▶ That's right. Monsieur Sellier will be seeing you at 11.15.

▷ **Could you tell me how to get to your office?**

▶ Don't worry. It's quite easy to find. Will you be coming by car?

▷ Yes. I hired a car at the airport.

▶ Réception, j'écoute.

▷ Ici la chambre 225. J'aimerais obtenir un numéro à l'extérieur.

▶ Certainement.

▷ C'est le 47 63 28 16.

▶ Ne quittez pas. Je fais le nécessaire.

〰〰〰〰

▶ Monsieur Brown, vous avez votre correspondant en ligne.

〰〰〰〰

▶ Allô?

▷ Bonjour, Mademoiselle. Roger Brown à l'appareil. **Je vous appelle pour confirmer mon rendez-vous** avec Monsieur Sellier.

▶ Oui, très bien. Monsieur Sellier vous recevra donc à 11h15.

▷ **Pourriez-vous m'indiquer comment me rendre à vos bureaux?**

▶ Ne vous inquiétez pas.[1] C'est facile à trouver. Vous êtes en voiture?

▷ Oui. J'ai loué une voiture à l'aéroport.

---

to make an outside call = *obtenir un numéro à l'extérieur*

to hire a car = *louer une voiture*

1. See notes 2 and 4 on page 33.

▶ *When you get to Versailles, follow the signs for the town centre. Carry straight on until you come to the second set of traffic lights, then turn left and our office is just opposite the Town Hall.*

▶ Lorsque vous arrivez à Versailles, prenez la direction 'Centre ville'. Continuez tout droit jusqu'au deuxième feu rouge, puis tournez à gauche et nos bureaux se trouvent juste en face de la Mairie.

▷ *Just a moment. **I'll have to write all that down.** Right, I follow the signs for the town centre, I carry straight on until the second set of traffic lights, then I turn left and your office is opposite the Town Hall.*

▷ Attendez. **Il faut que je note tout ça.** Alors, je prends la direction 'Centre ville', je continue tout droit jusqu'au deuxième feu rouge, puis je tourne à gauche et vos bureaux se trouvent en face de la Mairie.

▶ *Yes, that's right.*

▶ Oui, c'est ça.

▷ ***Is it easy to park nearby?***

▷ **On peut se garer facilement dans le quartier?**

▶ *No problem. There's a large paying car park just beside the office in Place de l'Orangerie.*

▶ Aucun problème. Il y a un grand parking payant sur la place de l'Orangerie juste à côté de nos bureaux.

▷ *OK.*

▷ D'accord.

▶ *The entrance to the building is on the corner of the street. Take the lift – we're on the fourth floor. And Monsieur Sellier's office is at the end of the corridor, on the right.*

▶ L'entrée de l'immeuble se trouve à l'angle de la rue. Prenez l'ascenseur – nous nous trouvons au quatrième étage. Et le bureau de Monsieur Sellier est au bout du couloir, à droite.

▷ *Oh dear. I hope I'll be able to find it. Thank you very much. **I'll see you in a little while.***

▷ Oh là là. J'espère que je vais trouver facilement. Merci beaucoup, Mademoiselle. **A tout à l'heure.**[1]

---

straight ahead = *tout droit*
left = *à gauche*
opposite = *en face de*
beside = *à côté de*
at the end of = *au bout de*
right = *à droite*

1. See note 5 on page 34.

☎〰〰〰 SUGGESTED ACTIVITIES

• Look at the signpost and practise giving someone directions, e.g. *Lorsque vous arrivez à Poitiers, prenez la direction 'Centre Ville'.*

• You could try using *il faut prendre . . .* and *il faut que vous preniez . . . .*

• If you were being given this information, how would you check it? e.g. *je prends la direction . . ., il faut que je prenne la direction . . . .*

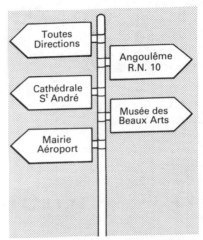

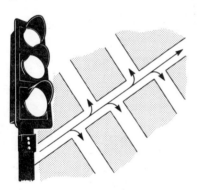

• Now do the same at the traffic lights, e.g. *au feu rouge, prenez la première rue à gauche.*

• Practise checking the directions being given too.

• Now try piecing together a whole sequence of instructions as in Dialogue 2.

☎〰〰〰 HOW WOULD YOU SAY IN FRENCH?

1 Don't take a taxi, take the RER.
2 Go and ask at reception.
3 It would be better to park in the square.
4 Our offices are on the ground floor.

Coup de fil

You are Peter or Pamela Simpson and you are ringing the Etablissements Baudin to confirm your appointment at 4 o'clock and to find out how to get to the office.

CHECKING AN
APPOINTMENT

TRAVEL DELAYS

☎〰〰〰 KEY PHRASES

I was due to meet you . . .	Je devais vous rencontrer . . .
I had an appointment with . . .	J'avais rendez-vous avec . . .
I'm ringing to let you know . . .	Je vous appelle pour vous prévenir . . .
I can't make it on time	Il me sera impossible d'être à l'heure
I will be late	Je serai en retard
I was an hour late for my appointment	J'avais une heure de retard sur mon rendez-vous
I'm running behind schedule	Je suis en retard sur mon horaire
Would it be possible for you to . . .	Vous serait-il possible de . . . ?
Will he still be able to see me?	Pourra-t-il toujours me recevoir?
Just a moment, let me check	Attendez, laissez-moi vérifier
Thank you very much	Je vous remercie
That's all right	Je vous en prie
That's very kind of you	C'est très gentil de votre part
You're welcome	Il n'y a pas de quoi
I am sorry	Je vous prie de m'excuser

DIALOGUE 1

▶ GMT, good morning.

▷ Monsieur Blanc, please.

▶ Sorry? The line is terribly bad. I can hardly hear you. Can you speak up?

▷ Monsieur Blanc, please.

▶ There's crackling on the line. Can you hear me? Can you ring back?

~~~~~~~

▶ Jean-Pierre Blanc speaking.

▷ Good morning, Monsieur Blanc. George Hunter here. **I was due to meet you** this morning at 11 o'clock.

▶ Yes, that's right.

▷ I am sorry, but **I'm not going to be able to make it on time.**

▶ I see.

▷ **I was already an hour late for my appointment** at 9 o'clock because there were roadworks on the motorway.

▶ GMT, bonjour.

▷ Monsieur Blanc, s'il vous plaît.

▶ Comment? La ligne est très mauvaise. Je vous entends à peine. Pouvez-vous parler plus fort?

▷ Monsieur Blanc, s'il vous plaît.

▶ Il y a des grésillements sur la ligne. Vous m'entendez? Pouvez-vous rappeler?

~~~~~~~

▶ Jean-Pierre Blanc à l'appareil.

▷ Bonjour Monsieur Blanc. George Hunter à l'appareil. **Je devais vous rencontrer** ce matin à 11 heures.

▶ Oui, en effet.

▷ Je suis désolé mais **il me sera impossible d'être à l'heure.**

▶ Ah bon.

▷ **J'avais**[1] **déjà une heure de retard sur mon rendez-vous** à 9 heures parce qu'il y avait[1] des travaux sur l'autoroute.

---

that's right = en effet
roadworks = des travaux

1. The imperfect tense is used, as here, to describe a situation in the past. See page 114 for the imperfect tense of regular verbs and page 116 for the irregular verbs.

▶ Yes. I understand. The traffic was awful this morning. It took me an hour and a half to get to work because of the traffic congestion.

▷ **I'm therefore running behind schedule. Would it be possible for you to** meet me at midday?

▶ No, I'm afraid not. I've a business lunch from 12 till 2 o'clock. **Just a moment, let me check.** The beginning of the afternoon is a bit difficult. I've already confirmed an appointment for 2 o'clock and I've promised to ring Gabon at 3.20. Could we say 4.15? Would that suit you?

▷ That's fine. I'll see you at 4.15 then. **Thank you very much, and I am sorry.**

▶ **That's all right.** I'll see you later.

▶ Oui, je comprends. La circulation était abominable ce matin. J'ai mis moi-même une heure et demie pour arriver à mon travail à cause des encombrements.

▷ **Je suis donc en retard sur mon horaire. Vous serait-il possible de** me rencontrer à midi?

▶ Ah non, malheureusement pas. J'ai accepté[1] un déjeuner d'affaires de midi à 14 heures. **Attendez . . . laissez-moi vérifier** . . . le début d'après-midi me paraît difficile. J'ai déjà confirmé[1] un rendez-vous à 14 heures et j'ai promis[1] d'appeler le Gabon[2] à 15h20. Disons 16h15? Cela vous convient?

▷ C'est parfait. A 16h15 alors. **Je vous remercie** et **je vous prie de m'excuser.**

▶ **Je vous en prie.** A plus tard.

---

the traffic = *la circulation*
because of = *à cause de*
to take an hour to do = *mettre une heure pour faire*
traffic congestion = *les encombrements*
a business lunch = *un déjeuner d'affaires*

1. The perfect tense can be used, as here, to list actions in the past. Note the difference between this and the use of the imperfect tense. See page 115 for the perfect tense.

2. *Le Gabon*, e.g. *il travaille au Gabon*.

DIALOGUE 2

Please wait, all the lines are engaged.

Please wait, all the lines are engaged.

Veuillez patienter, toutes les lignes de votre correspondant sont occupées.
Veuillez patienter, toutes les lignes de votre correspondant sont occupées.

▶ *Textiles Fauchard, good morning.*

▷ *Gaston Deschamps, please.*

▶ *May I ask who's calling?*

▷ *Richard Davies.*

▶ *Hold on please. I'll see if he can take the call.*

〰〰〰〰〰

▶ *Hello, Mr Davies. Monsieur Deschamps is in a meeting at the moment. Can he ring you back when he's free?*

▷ *No, he can't. I'm at the airport. Can you put me through to his secretary? It's urgent.*

▶ *Yes, of course.*

〰〰〰〰〰

▶ *Hello, Mr Davies. She's on a call. Do you want to hold?*

▷ *Look, I'm ringing from a phone box and . . .*

▶ *Ah, she's free now.*

〰〰〰〰〰

▶ *Françoise Fortin.*

▷ *Good morning. Richard Davies speaking. **I had an appointment with** Monsieur Deschamps at 11.30.*

▶ *Yes, that's right.*

▶ Textiles Fauchard, bonjour.

▷ Gaston Deschamps, s'il vous plaît.

▶ C'est de la part de qui?

▷ Richard Davies.

▶ Ne quittez pas. Je vais voir s'il peut prendre la communication.

〰〰〰〰〰

▶ Allô, Monsieur Davies. Monsieur Deschamps est actuellement en réunion. Il peut vous rappeler dès qu'il sera libre?

▷ Non, non, je suis à l'aéroport. Pouvez-vous me passer sa secrétaire. C'est urgent.

▶ Oui, bien sûr.

〰〰〰〰〰

▶ Allô, Monsieur Davies. Son poste est occupé. Vous voulez patienter?

▷ Ecoutez. Je téléphone d'une cabine téléphonique et . . .

▶ Ah, elle est libre maintenant.

〰〰〰〰〰

▶ Françoise Fortin.

▷ Bonjour Madame. Richard Davies à l'appareil. **J'avais rendez-vous avec** Monsieur Deschamps à 11h30.

▶ Oui, en effet.

a strike = *une grève*
a telephone box = *une cabine téléphonique*

▷ *I'm ringing to let you know that I'll be late.*

▶ *I see.*

▷ *I've just arrived. There's an air traffic controllers' strike and all the flights have been delayed. Oh dear. I've only got 40 centimes left.*

▶ *Oh, you're in a phone box. Give me the number.*

▷ *Em . . . Oh, yes. It's 45 43 21 58.*

▶ *Put the receiver down and I'll ring you back straight away.*

〜〜〜〜〜〜

▶ *Hello, Monsieur Davies.*

▷ *Yes, **thank you very much**. I didn't have any more change.*

▶ ***That's all right**. Now, you'll be late, is that right?*

▷ *Yes, I'm still in Paris so I've missed my connection at 9.10. I've made enquiries and the next flight's at 10.20 getting in at 11.40. I'll therefore be about an hour late arriving in Toulouse.*

▶ *OK. You'll be an hour late.*

▷ **Je vous appelle pour vous prévenir** que **je serai en retard.**

▶ Ah bon.

▷ Je viens juste d'arriver. Il y a une grève des contrôleurs aériens et tous les vols ont été retardés. Oh là là. Il ne me reste que 40 centimes.

▶ Ah, vous êtes dans une cabine téléphonique. Donnez-moi le numéro.

▷ Euh! Ah, oui. C'est le 45 43 21 58.

▶ Raccrochez. Je vous rappelle tout de suite.

〜〜〜〜〜〜

▶ Allô, Monsieur Davies.

▷ Oui. Merci. **Je vous remercie.**[1] Je n'avais plus de monnaie.

▶ **Je vous en prie.**[1] Alors vous serez en retard, dites-vous.

▷ Oui. Je suis toujours à Paris. J'ai donc raté la correspondance de 9h10. Je me suis renseigné et le prochain vol est à 10h20, arrivée 11h40. J'arriverai donc à Toulouse avec à peu près une heure de retard.

▶ D'accord. Vous aurez une heure de retard.

---

the flights have been delayed = *les vols ont été retardés*
I've only got . . . left = *il ne me reste que . . .*
I didn't have any more change = *Je n'avais plus de monnaie*
to miss the connection = *rater la correspondance*
to make enquiries = *se renseigner*

1. Thanking is very important, so too is the response to being thanked, particularly on the phone when smiles and nods can't be seen.

▷ Yes. **Will Monsieur Deschamps still be able to see me** at 12.30?

▶ Yes. I think so. He hasn't anything arranged for then. What's the number of your flight?

▷ IT 475.

▶ Good. Someone will come and meet you at the airport.

▷ **That's really very kind of you.**

▶ You're welcome. We'll see you later then. Bye.

▷ Oui. Monsieur Deschamps **pourra-t-il toujours me recevoir** à midi et demi?

▶ Je pense que oui. Il n'a rien de prévu à cette heure-là. Quel est le numéro de votre vol?

▷ IT 475.

▶ Très bien. Quelqu'un viendra vous chercher à l'aéroport.

▷ **C'est très gentil de votre part,**[1] Madame.

▶ **Il n'y a pas de quoi,**[1] Monsieur. A plus tard. Au revoir.

to come and meet = *venir chercher*

☎〰〰〰〰 SUGGESTED ACTIVITIES

• The five people in the telephone boxes are ringing from the airport to explain that they will be late for their appointments.

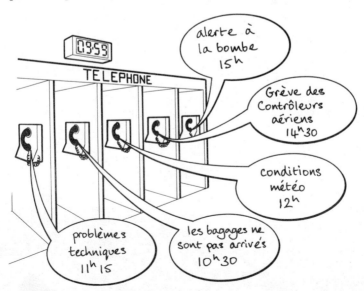

• Practise starting off their telephone calls, using *je devais vous rencontrer à . . . .*

• Try explaining why they are late. Use *parce que* + verb and/or *à cause de* + noun, as appropriate.

• Now go through each of the conversations from the beginning and finish them off.

🕿〰〰〰〰 **HOW WOULD YOU SAY IN FRENCH?**

1 He made enquiries.
2 Would it be possible for you to see me at 4 o'clock?
3 She took an hour and a half to get to work.
4 I've just arrived.

Coup de fil

You're ringing Madame Foch to explain you're an hour behind schedule and to find out if it's still going to be possible to meet.

UNIT 7

REARRANGING AN APPOINTMENT

HOTELS AND HIRED CARS

☎〰〰〰〰 KEY PHRASES

I will not be able to meet you as we'd arranged	Je ne pourrai pas vous rencontrer comme nous l'avions convenu
I'm going to have to stay in . . .	Je vais être obligé de m'arrêter à . . .
Is it possible to change the dates?	Serait-il possible de changer les dates?
Could you put back the appointment?	Pourriez-vous repousser le rendez-vous?
I can move the appointment back	Je peux reculer le rendez-vous
Could you arrange it all?	Pourriez-vous faire le nécessaire?
That's no problem	Cela ne pose aucun problème
We're still talking about . . . aren't we?	Il s'agit toujours de . . . , n'est-ce pas?
Have you had a good trip?	Vous avez fait bon voyage?

DIALOGUE 1

▶ *Hello.*

▷ *Madame Durand?*

▶ *Speaking.*

▷ *Good morning. Peter Duncan speaking.*

▶ *Good morning, Mr Duncan.* **Did you have a good journey?**

▷ *Well, no. I didn't. I had an accident yesterday evening on the motorway.*

▶ *An accident! What happened?*

▷ *It was all because of the fog. The weather was just awful – visibility was down to 10 metres. And suddenly I crashed into another car.*

▶ *Oh dear me. You aren't hurt, are you?*

▷ *No, I was lucky. I'm OK but the car's a write-off.*

▶ *Oh my goodness!*

▷ *I'm very sorry, I'm afraid* **I won't be able to meet you** *this morning* **as we'd arranged.**

▶ Allô.

▷ Madame Durand?

▶ Oui, elle-même.

▷ Bonjour, Madame. Peter Duncan à l'appareil.

▶ Ah bonjour, Monsieur Duncan. **Vous avez fait bon voyage?**

▷ Euh non. Pas du tout. J'ai eu un accident hier soir sur l'autoroute.

▶ Un accident! Qu'est-ce qui s'est passé?

▷ C'est à cause du brouillard. Il faisait[1] vraiment un temps affreux – la visibilité ne dépassait pas 10 mètres. Et tout à coup je suis entré en collision avec une autre voiture.

▶ Mon Dieu! Vous n'êtes pas blessé?

▷ Non, j'ai eu de la chance, je ne suis pas blessé mais la voiture est bonne pour la ferraille.

▶ Oh quelle histoire!

▷ Je suis sincèrement désolé mais **je ne pourrai pas vous rencontrer** ce matin **comme nous l'avions convenu.**

What happened? = *Qu'est-ce qui s'est passé?*
The weather was awful = *Il faisait un temps affreux*
suddenly = *tout à coup*
to be lucky = *avoir de la chance*
Oh my goodness = *Quelle histoire!*

1. *faire* is used with several expressions to describe the weather, e.g. *il fait beau, il fait du soleil, il fait lourd.*

▶ But you are still planning to come to Lyon, aren't you?

▶ Vous avez toujours l'intention de venir à Lyon, n'est-ce pas?

▷ Yes, I am. **Could you put our appointment off** until tomorrow morning?

▷ Oui. **Pourriez-vous repousser notre rendez-vous** jusqu'à demain matin?

▶ *That's no problem. I can move the appointment back* to . . . let's see . . . I can offer you 10 o'clock or 11 o'clock. Does that suit you?

▶ **Cela ne pose aucun problème. Je peux reculer le rendez-vous** jusqu'à . . . Voyons . . . je peux vous proposer 10h ou 11h. Cela vous convient?

▷ 10 o'clock is fine. That's very kind of you.

▷ 10 heures. C'est parfait. C'est très gentil, Madame.

▶ You're welcome.

▶ Il n'y a pas de quoi.

▷ By the way, Madame Durand. I'd like to hire a car at the airport to get to Dijon but I don't get in to Lyon until 10 o'clock at night. **Could you arrange it all** with a car hire company?

▷ Dites-donc, Madame Durand. J'aimerais louer une voiture à l'aéroport pour me rendre à Dijon mais je n'arrive à Lyon qu'à 10 heures du soir. **Pourriez-vous faire le nécessaire** auprès d'une compagnie de location?

▶ Of course. What sort of car do you want?

▶ Bien sûr. Vous voulez quel type de voiture?

▷ It doesn't matter. It doesn't make any difference. A Renault 19, let's say.

▷ N'importe. Cela m'est égal. Une Renault 19, par exemple.

▶ And for how long?

▶ Et pour combien de jours?

▷ The whole week. From the 19th to the 26th.

▷ La semaine entière. Du 19 au 26.

▶ From the 19th to the 26th. Don't worry – I'll see to everything.

▶ Du 19 au 26. Ne vous inquiétez pas – je m'occupe de tout.

▷ That's very good of you.

▷ C'est très aimable à vous.[1]

It doesn't matter = n'importe
It doesn't make any difference = Cela
m'est égal
I'll see to everything = Je m'occupe de tout

1. Another way to thank and reply.

▶ *That's all right. We'll see you tomorrow then.*

▷ *Yes, I'll see you tomorrow and thank you once again.*

▶ Je vous en prie. A demain donc.

▷ A demain, et merci encore.

DIALOGUE 2

▶ *Hotel Aquitania, good morning.*

▷ *Good morning. My secretary rang you last week to reserve a room.*

▶ *Who was the booking made for?*

▷ *Shepherd, Paul Shepherd.*

▶ *Just a moment, I'll check. What name did you say?*

▷ *Shepherd.* SHEPHERD.

▶ *Yes, here it is. Room 503. The room was booked for 2 nights – the 18th and 19th.*

▷ *That's right. I'm ringing to let you know that I won't be able to make Bordeaux this evening. **I'm going to have to stay** in Tours tonight and I won't be arriving in Bordeaux now until tomorrow morning. **Would it be possible** to change the dates of the booking?*

▶ Hôtel Aquitania, bonjour.

▷ Bonjour, Mademoiselle. Ma secrétaire vous a téléphoné la semaine dernière pour réserver une chambre.

▶ La réservation a été faite[1] à quel nom?

▷ Shepherd, Paul Shepherd.

▶ Attendez, je vérifie. Quel nom avez-vous dit?

▷ Shepherd. SHEPHERD.

▶ Oui, voilà. Chambre 503. La chambre a été réservée[1] pour deux nuits – les 18 et 19.

▷ En effet. Je vous appelle pour vous prévenir que je ne pourrai pas être à Bordeaux ce soir. **Je vais être obligé[1] de m'arrêter** ce soir à Tours et je n'arriverai à Bordeaux que demain matin. **Serait-il possible de changer les dates** de la réservation?

---

1. 'The room **was booked** by my secretary'. This is referred to as a passive construction. See page 114 for the pattern. You will notice agreements with this construction which are important in written French, but which are not always noticeable in the spoken language.

▶ I'll have to check but I don't think so. With the Trade Fair all our rooms have been booked in advance. Please hold.

▷ OK.

▶ Hello? You're lucky. The booking for room 125 hasn't been confirmed. So we can say room 125 for the 19th and 20th, Mr Shepherd.

▷ That's a relief. **We are still talking about** a single room with private facilities, **aren't we.**

▶ Yes – a single room with a private bathroom at 350 francs a night. Breakfast is not included.

▷ That's fine. Thank you very much. Goodbye.

▶ Je dois vérifier, Monsieur, mais je ne pense pas. Avec la Foire-Exposition, toutes nos chambres ont été réservées[1] à l'avance. Restez en ligne, s'il vous plaît.

▷ D'accord.

▶ Allô? Vous avez de la chance. La réservation de la chambre 125 n'a pas été confirmée.[1] Alors nous disons donc chambre 125 pour les nuits du 19 et du 20, Monsieur Shepherd.

▷ Vous me rassurez. **Il s'agit toujours d'**une chambre simple avec salle de bains, **n'est-ce pas?**

▶ Oui, Monsieur – chambre simple, avec salle de bains privée. 350F la nuit. Le petit déjeuner est en supplément.

▷ Très bien, Mademoiselle. Je vous remercie. Au revoir.

That's a relief = *Vous me rassurez*
a single room = *une chambre simple*
with private facilities = *avec salle de bains*
not included = *en supplément*

☎〜〜〜 SUGGESTED ACTIVITIES

- Looking at the calendar you'll notice some dates have been blocked off.

AVRIL

Lu		4	11	18	25
Ma		5	12	19	26
Me		6	13	20	27
Je		7	14	21	28
Ve	1	8	15	22	29
Sa	2	9	16	23	30
Di	3	10	17	24	

MAI

Lu		2	9	16	23	30
Ma		3	10	17	24	31
Me		4	11	18	25	
Je		5	12	19	26	
Ve		6	13	20	27	
Sa		7	14	21	28	
Di	1	8	15	22	29	

JUIN

Lu		6	13	20	27
Ma		7	14	21	28
Me	1	8	15	22	29
Je	2	9	16	23	30
Ve	3	10	17	24	
Sa	4	11	18	25	
Di	5	12	19	26	

JUILLET

Lu		4	11	18	25
Ma		5	12	19	26
Me		6	13	20	27
Je		7	14	21	28
Ve	1	8	15	22	29
Sa	2	9	16	23	30
Di	3	10	17	24	31

AOUT

Lu	1	8	15	22	29
Ma	2	9	16	23	30
Me	3	10	17	24	31
Je	4	11	18	25	
Ve	5	12	19	26	
Sa	6	13	20	27	
Di	7	14	21	28	

SEPTEMBRE

Lu		5	12	19	26
Ma		6	13	20	27
Me		7	14	21	28
Je	1	8	15	22	29
Ve	2	9	16	23	30
Sa	3	10	17	24	
Di	4	11	18	25	

OCTOBRE

Lu		3	10	17	24	31
Ma		4	11	18	25	
Me		5	12	19	26	
Je		6	13	20	27	
Ve		7	14	21	28	
Sa	1	8	15	22	29	
Di	2	9	16	23	30	

NOVEMBRE

Lu		7	14	21	28
Ma	1	8	15	22	29
Me	2	9	16	23	30
Je	3	10	17	24	
Ve	4	11	18	25	
Sa	5	12	19	26	
Di	6	13	20	27	

- Practise saying out loud the first and last date of each block, e.g. *le 7 avril*.

- Describe the length of the block using *du . . . au . . .*: 'from . . . to . . .' e.g. *du 7 au 9 avril*.

- Add time phrases with *pour* to describe the whole block, e.g. *pour la semaine entière, pour cinq jours, pour quinze jours*.

- Try booking a single room for those periods with a bath or shower (*une douche*). Find out how much it is a night and if breakfast is included (*compris*) or extra (*en supplément*).

- Imagine you're trying to change these bookings. Find out if it would be possible and work out some new dates.

☎〜〜〜 HOW WOULD YOU SAY IN FRENCH?

1 I intend coming to Paris tomorrow.
2 The reservation was made last week.
3 I've hired a car to get to the Trade Fair.
4 Don't worry, that's no problem.

Coup de fil

You are Angela/Andrew Watson and you're ringing to rearrange the appointment you have with Madame Alibert.

CANCELLING AN APPOINTMENT

TRAVEL ARRANGEMENTS

📞〰〰〰〰 KEY PHRASES

I'd rather speak to him/her personally	Je préfère lui parler personnellement
We were due to meet . . .	Nous devions nous rencontrer . . .
Something's cropped up at the last minute	J'ai un empêchement de dernière minute
I have to cancel this appointment	Je suis obligé d'annuler ce rendez-vous
Is there nothing else you can do?	Vous ne pouvez pas faire autrement?
It's essential that I am . . .	Il est indispensable que je sois . . .
I have to be at a meeting	Il faut que j'assiste à une réunion
I'm really very sorry Please accept my apologies	Je regrette infiniment Veuillez accepter toutes mes excuses
You'd better take . . .	Il vaut mieux que vous preniez . . .
Can you give me the time of the next train?	Pouvez-vous me donner l'horaire du prochain train?

DIALOGUE 1

▶ *Sonnex, good afternoon.*

▷ *Could you put me through to Monsieur Leroy, please.*

▶ *He's on a call. I can put you through to his secretary if you like.*

▷ *No, I'll just wait. **I'd rather speak to him personally.***

〰〰〰〰

▶ *Hello, Leroy speaking.*

▷ *Michael Cook here. My secretary contacted you a fortnight ago. **We were due to meet** tomorrow at 10.30.*

▶ *Yes.*

▷ *I'm really sorry but **I have to cancel this appointment**. I absolutely have to go back to London this morning.*

▶ Sonnex, bonjour.

▷ Pourriez-vous me passer Monsieur Leroy, s'il vous plaît.

▶ Il est en ligne. Je peux vous passer sa secrétaire, si vous le désirez?

▷ Non, non. Je patiente. **Je préfère lui parler personnellement.**

〰〰〰〰

▶ Allô, Leroy à l'appareil.

▷ Ici Michael Cook. Ma secrétaire vous a contacté il y a quinze jours. **Nous devions nous rencontrer** demain à 10h30.

▶ Oui.

▷ Je suis vraiment désolé mais **je suis obligé d'annuler ce rendez-vous.** Je dois absolument retourner à Londres ce matin même.

---

a fortnight ago = *il y a quinze jours*

▶ *That's a shame. **Is there nothing else you can do?** There's a lot we have to go over together.*

▶ Quel dommage! **Vous ne pouvez pas faire autrement?** Nous avons beaucoup de choses à[1] voir ensemble.

▷ *I'm afraid not. **It's essential I'm** back in London in the course of the morning to get something important sorted out. **I am extremely sorry.***

▷ Malheureusement non. **Il est indispensable que je sois**[2] à Londres dans le courant de la matinée pour[3] régler une affaire importante. **Je regrette infiniment.**

▶ *But you are planning to come back to Paris in the near future, aren't you?*

▶ Vous comptez revenir prochainement à Paris?

▷ *Yes, I think so. Definitely before the end of the month.*

▷ Je pense que oui. Avant la fin du mois certainement.

▶ *Yes, because we must get together to finalise the details of our contract.*

▶ Oui, parce qu'il est nécessaire que nous nous rencontrions[2] enfin pour[3] mettre au point les détails de notre contrat.

▷ *Yes, of course. My secretary will contact you tomorrow to make a new appointment.*

▷ Oui, oui, bien sûr. Ma secrétaire vous contactera demain pour[3] prendre un nouveau rendez-vous.

▶ *Very good.*

▶ Très bien.

▷ ***Please accept my apologies.***

▷ **Veuillez accepter toutes mes excuses.**

▶ *That's all right. Goodbye, Mr Cook. We'll see you soon.*

▶ Je vous en prie. Au revoir, Monsieur Cook. A bientôt.

---

that's a shame/what a pity = *quel dommage*
in the course of the morning = *dans le courant de la matinée*
to look at/to go over = *voir*
to sort out a matter = *régler une affaire*
Are you planning . . . ? = *Vous comptez . . . ?*
in the near future = *prochainement*
I think so = *Je pense que oui*
to get together/to meet = *se rencontrer*
to finalise = *mettre au point*

1. *avoir quelque chose à faire* = to have something to do, e.g. 'we have things to go over', 'I have a plane to catch'.

2. *Il est indispensable que . . .*, *il est nécessaire que . . .* and *il vaut mieux que . . .* are all followed by the subjunctive.

3. *pour* + infinitive means 'in order to'.

DIALOGUE 2

▶ *SNCF, good morning.*

▷ *Good morning. I'd like to know if . . .*

▶ *You're through to Reservations.*

▷ *I'd just like to know if . . .*

▶ *You have to ring 80 17 23 90 for Enquiries.*

▷ *Ah. OK.*

〰〰〰〰〰

▶ *Enquiries, can I help you?*

▷ *Good morning. I was due to take the TGV for Paris at 12.36 but **something's cropped up at the last minute. I have to be at a** meeting at the end of the morning and I'm therefore going to miss the train.*

▶ *Yes.*

▷ *I think I'll be free at the beginning of the afternoon. **Can you give me the time of the next train**, please?*

▶ *You have several. One which leaves at 14.48 and gets in at 16.28. The next one leaves at 16.55 and arrives at 18.35. The one after that leaves at 18.34 and arrives at 20.19.*

▶ SNCF, bonjour.

▷ Bonjour, Madame. Je voudrais savoir si . . .

▶ Vous êtes au service des réservations, Monsieur.

▷ Je voudrais simplement savoir si . . .

▶ Pour les renseignements, vous devez faire le 80 17 23 90.

▷ Ah! Bon.

〰〰〰〰〰

▶ Renseignements, j'écoute.

▷ Bonjour, Monsieur. Je devais prendre le TGV[1] de 12h36, à destination de Paris mais **j'ai un empêchement de dernière minute. Il faut que j'assiste à** une réunion en fin de matinée et je vais donc rater le train.

▶ Oui.

▷ Euh, je pense que je serai libre en début d'après-midi. **Pouvez-vous me donner l'horaire du prochain train**, s'il vous plaît?

▶ Vous en avez plusieurs.
  Départ 14h48   Arrivée 16h28
  Départ 16h55   Arrivée 18h35
  Départ 18h34   Arrivée 20h19.

---

you have to ring = *vous devez faire le . . .*
to miss the train = *rater le train*
time (of trains) = *l'horaire*

1. *Le Train à Grande Vitesse*. France's high speed trains.

▷ 14.48 is a bit tight. The one at 18.34 gets in at what time again?

▶ 20.19.

▷ No, that's too late. It's essential I'm at Roissy around 9 o'clock as I've a plane to catch and it'll take over an hour to get to the airport.

▶ In that case, **you'd better take the one at 16.55.**

▷ Arriving at what time, did you say?

▶ It gets in to Paris, Gare de Lyon at 18.35.

▷ That's fine. Do I have to make a new reservation?

▶ Yes, you do. Reservations are compulsory.

▷ Can I make the reservation by phone?

▶ Yes, if you ring Reservations. The number is 80 93 37 74.

▷ 14h48, c'est un peu juste. Celui de 18h34 arrive à quelle heure?

▶ 20h19.

▷ Non, c'est trop tard. Il est indispensable que je sois[1] à Roissy vers 21 heures car j'ai un avion à[2] prendre et il faut plus d'une heure pour aller à l'aéroport.

▶ Dans ce cas, Monsieur, **il vaut mieux que vous preniez**[1] celui de 16h55.

▷ Arrivée à quelle heure, avez-vous dit?

▶ Arrivée Paris, Gare de Lyon à 18h35.

▷ C'est parfait. Est-ce que je dois réserver de nouveau?

▶ Ah oui, Monsieur, c'est obligatoire.

▷ Je peux effectuer la réservation par téléphone?

▶ Oui, Monsieur, au service des réservations. Vous faites le 80 93 37 74.

---

a bit tight = *un peu juste*
to catch a plane = *prendre un avion*
to make a reservation = *effectuer une réservation*

1. See note 2 on page 53.
2. See note 1 on page 53.

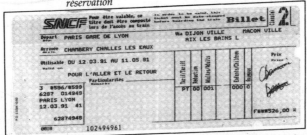

☎〜〜〜〜 **SUGGESTED ACTIVITIES**

• Revise the numbers and time in Units 2 and 3 respectively if you feel unsure about coping with train times.

🔘● Listen to the tape and note down the departure and arrival times and the train numbers of the trains between Paris and Brussels.

Train No.				
Paris-Nord				
St Quentin	9.11	15.07	17.57	1.20
Mons	10.08	16.04	18.51	3.51
Bruxelles-Midi				

☎〜〜〜〜 **HOW WOULD YOU SAY IN FRENCH?**

1 He was due to meet you at the end of the morning.
2 I've an important matter to sort out.
3 She's sorry, she has to cancel the appointment.
4 I'm terribly sorry. There's nothing else I can do.

Coup de fil

You're Richard/Rachel Martin and you're ringing Monsieur Bordier to explain that you're going to have to cancel your meeting with him.

REVIEW

THIS IS A RECORDED MESSAGE ...

Vous êtes en communication avec le répondeur automatique des Etablissements Charrier. Nos bureaux sont ouverts tous les jours sauf le dimanche de 7h30 à 12h et de 14h à 18h. Si vous le désirez, vous pouvez laisser un message après le bip sonore. Merci de votre appel.

Oui, bonjour. Jack Stanley à l'appareil.
Monsieur Bruel pourrait-il me rappeler dès que possible.
C'est au sujet de la réunion à Sheffield, le semaine prochaine.
Mon numéro de téléphone est le 742 4739.
Merci.

La Maison Phocéenne, bonjour. En raison du pont du 15 août, nos bureaux seront fermés du samedi 12 au mercredi 16 au matin. Veuillez laisser votre nom et votre numéro de téléphone. Nous vous rappellerons. Merci et bon week-end.

• Practise leaving messages for the following situations. There are some suggestions as to what you might say on the next page.

1 You'd like to meet Madame Bouvard sometime next week. Give your name and the name of your company. Could she ring you back as soon as possible. The number is 792 567431.

2 Leave your name and the company's name. Confirm you will be arriving at Marseilles-Marignane Monday 21st August at 10.45 on British Airways flight no. BA 782. Ask if Monsieur Fauré can come and meet you.

3 Give your name. Explain you are going to have to cancel the appointment you had on Friday 18th at 2.15 pm. Explain you will call back on 16th to arrange another appointment.

SAMPLE MESSAGES

1 *Je suis .... de ....*
Je voudrais rencontrer Madame Bouvard dans le courant de la semaine prochaine. Pourrait-elle me rappeler au bureau dès que possible. Le numéro est le suivant: 792 567431.

2 *M..........*
Je vous appelle pour confirmer mon arrivée à l'aéroport de Marseille-Marignane, le lundi 21 août. C'est le vol British Airways, no. BA 782 à 10h45. Monsieur Fauré pourrait-il venir me chercher, s'il vous plaît. Merci.

3 *M..........*
J'ai un empêchement de dernière minute et je vais être obligé(e) d'annuler notre rendez-vous du vendredi 18 août à 14h15. Je vous rappellerai le 16 pour fixer un autre rendez-vous.

CHECKLIST

Can you now do the following:

1 Spell your own name and your company's name?

2 Give your telephone number and code in French?

3 Ask someone to repeat a name or a number?

4 Ask someone to speak
(a) more slowly because you haven't quite understood?
(b) more loudly because the line's bad and you can hardly hear them?

5 Confirm, rearrange, cancel a meeting?

6 In two different ways,
(a) thank someone and respond if you are thanked?
(b) apologise?

GETTING INFORMATION

WHO'S WHO

☎ KEY PHRASES

I would like to receive . . .	Je voudrais recevoir . . .
Could you send me . . .	Pourriez-vous m'envoyer . . .
I'd like some information on . . .	J'aimerais avoir des renseignements sur . . .
	Je voudrais des renseignements concernant . . .
Could you give me the details of where to send it?	Pourriez-vous me donner vos coordonnées?
Just a moment, let me write that down	Attendez, je note
I'll send it off to you	Je vous l'envoie
I'll send you our catalogue	Je vous fais parvenir notre catalogue
Can I help you?	Puis-je vous renseigner?
Could you put me through to someone who can help me?	Pourriez-vous me passer la personne concernée?
She's the person to talk to	Elle sera à même de vous répondre
I'm the technical director	Je suis directeur technique
I'm in charge of sales	Je suis le responsable des ventes
He works in the sales department	Il travaille au service des ventes

DIALOGUE 1

▷ *Monsieur . . . um . . . Canteloup, please.*

▷ Monsieur . . . euh . . . Canteloup, s'il vous plaît.

▶ *Monsieur Canteloup. There's no-one of that name in our company.*

▶ Monsieur Canteloup. Il n'y a personne de ce nom dans notre entreprise.

▷ *But **he works in the sales department.** I spoke to him last week.*

▷ Mais **il travaille au service des ventes.** Je lui ai parlé la semaine dernière.

▶ *Do you know how it's spelt?*

▶ Vous savez comment cela s'écrit?

▷ *Yes, just a moment. I've got his business card here.* CANTELOUP.

▷ Oui, attendez. J'ai sa carte de visite ici. CANTELOUP.

▶ *Oh, Monsieur Canteloup! Yes, just hold on a moment please. I'll put you through to him.*

▶ Ah, Monsieur Canteloup! Oui, oui, ne quittez pas. Je vous le passe.

〰〰〰〰

〰〰〰〰

▶ *Hello, yes, can I help you?*

▶ Allô, oui, j'écoute.

▷ *Good morning. David Smith speaking. I work for a British company called Pepco. **I'm in charge of sales.***

▷ Bonjour, Monsieur. David Smith à l'appareil. Je travaille pour une compagnie britannique, Pepco. **Je suis le responsable des ventes.**[1]

▶ *Oh yes, you were at the Trade Fair in Marseille last week, weren't you.*

▶ Ah oui, vous étiez[2] à la Foire Exposition de Marseille la semaine dernière.

---

the company = *l'entreprise*
his business card = *sa carte de visite*

1. You'll find a diagram of a company structure with departments on page 122.

2. Imperfect tense of *être* (see page 116) used here to describe something in the past and to be contrasted with *j'ai visité* in the perfect tense, used here to pinpoint action in the past.

▷ *That's right. I had a look at your stand which I found very interesting.*

▶ *That's good.*

▷ *I've got the company literature which your representative gave me here in front of me.* **I'd like to have some information on your prices. Could you send me** *a copy of your price list?*

▶ *Of course. If you'd care to give me the details of where to send it. Do you have a fax machine? That would be faster.*

▷ *Yes. The fax number is 21 632 4775.*

▶ *Let me repeat that – 632 4765.*

▷ *No, not 65, 75.*

▶ *632 4775 and the code is 21, is that right?*

▷ *Yes, that's it.*

▶ *Well, then, that's fine.* **I'll send it off to you** *straight away.*

▷ *Thank you very much. Bye.*

▶ *That's all right. You're welcome. Bye.*

▷ En effet, j'ai visité[1] votre stand qui[2] m'a beaucoup intéressé.

▶ Très bien.

▷ J'ai sous les yeux la documentation que[2] m'a donnée votre représentant. **J'aimerais avoir des renseignements sur** vos tarifs. **Pourriez-vous m'envoyer** votre liste de prix?

▶ Avec plaisir. Si vous voulez bien me donner vos coordonnées. Vous avez un télécopieur? Ce sera plus rapide.

▷ Oui, le numéro de fax est le 21 632 47 75.

▶ Je répète, 632 47 65.

▷ Non, non, pas 65, 75.

▶ 632 47 75 et l'indicatif est le 21, c'est ça?

▷ Oui, c'est ça.

▶ Bon, très bien. **Je vous l'envoie** tout de suite.

▷ Je vous remercie,[3] Monsieur. Au revoir.

▶ A votre service,[3] Monsieur. Au revoir.

---

company literature = *la documentation*
in front of me = *sous les yeux*
your prices/rates = *vos tarifs*
your price list = *votre liste de prix*
details (of where to send something) or of how and where to get in touch with someone = *vos coordonnées*
a fax machine = *un télécopieur*
immediately/straight away = *tout de suite*

1. See note 2 on page 60.

2. *qui/que* can both be translated here by 'which'. *Qui* is the subject of the verb, *que* is the object.

3. Notice how they say thank you. See page 125.

DIALOGUE 2

▷ *GTA Ltd., can I help you?*

▶ *Good morning. Do you speak French?*

▷ *Yes, a little.*

▶ *Well, I'm ringing from Marseilles. **I'd like some information on** your products. **Could you put me through to someone who can help me?***

▷ *I'll put you through to Mrs Barron, our sales manager. **She's the person to talk to.** Just hold on please.*

〰〰〰〰〰

▷ *Hello.*

▶ *Good morning. Georges Aubert speaking. I'm ringing from Marseilles. **I'm the technical director** at Phoenix.*

▷ *Yes. **Can I help you?***

▶ *Yes. I'm very interested in the products your company manufactures and **I'd like to receive** a copy of your catalogue.*

▷ *Yes, of course. **Could you give me the details of where to send it,** please?*

▶ *The company is Phoenix S.A.*

▷ ***Just a moment, let me write that down.** Phoenix. Could you spell that?*

▷ GTA Ltd., can I help you?

▶ Bonjour, Mademoiselle. Vous parlez français?

▷ Oui, un peu.

▶ Je vous téléphone de Marseille. **Je voudrais des renseignements concernant** vos produits. **Pourriez-vous me passer la personne concernée?**

▷ Je vous passe Mrs Barron, notre directeur[1] des ventes. **Elle sera à même de vous répondre.** Ne quittez pas.

〰〰〰〰〰

▷ Allô.

▶ Bonjour, Georges Aubert à l'appareil. Je vous téléphone de Marseille. **Je suis directeur technique** chez Phoenix.

▷ Oui. **Puis-je vous renseigner?**

▶ Oui. Je suis très intéressé par les produits fabriqués par votre compagnie et **je voudrais recevoir** votre catalogue.

▷ Mais oui, bien sûr. **Pourriez-vous me donner vos coordonnées, s'il vous plaît?**

▶ C'est Phoenix S.A.

▷ **Attendez, je note.** Phoenix. Pourriez-vous épeler cela?

---

to make/manufacture = *fabriquer*

1. You will also hear *directrice des ventes.*

▶ PHOENIX.

▷ Oh, Phoenix! Yes, and the address?

▶ The address is as follows: 16 avenue du Quatre Septembre, 13184 Marseilles. Cedex 12.

▷ Could you repeat the post code, please?

▶ 13184.

▷ 13124.

▶ No, 84.

▷ 13184. I'm sorry, my French is not very good.

▶ Oh yes it is. You're managing very well.

▷ Thank you. Well, **I'll send you our catalogue** today.

▶ That's very kind of you. Thank you.

▷ You're welcome. Bye.

▶ PHOENIX.

▷ Ah Phoenix! Oui, et l'adresse?

▶ L'adresse est la suivante: 16 avenue du Quatre Septembre, 13184 Marseille. Cedex 12.

▷ Pourriez-vous répéter le code postal, s'il vous plaît?

▶ 13184.

▷ 13124.

▶ Non, Madame, 84.

▷ 13184. Excusez-moi, je ne parle pas très bien français.

▶ Mais si.[1] Vous vous débrouillez[2] très bien.

▷ Merci. Alors, **je vous fais parvenir notre catalogue** aujourd'hui-même.

▶ C'est très gentil de votre part.[3]

▷ Je vous en prie,[3] Monsieur. Au revoir.

My French is not very good = *je ne parle pas très bien français*
to cope/manage = *se débrouiller*
That's very kind of you = *C'est très gentil de votre part*
You're welcome = *Je vous en prie*

1. *Si* is used for 'yes' in reply to a negative question or statement.

2. See page 119 for the reflexive verbs.

3. See note 3 on page 61.

🕿 〰〰〰〰 SUGGESTED ACTIVITIES

Claude Marnat
Directeur des ventes
CMD
28, Place Richelieu   téléphone: 56.00.24
59140 Dunkerque   télécopie: 65.18.18

Téléphone (1) 69.36.16.00
Télex 135.537 F
PATRICK VAIRONT   DELTA FRANCE
92 Avenue Victor Hugo   Gérant
BP 38
91360 Montgeron

JACQUES PRADOUX
responsable commercial

GARONEXPORT

113 bd de la Somme
31200 Toulouse Cedex 10
telephone: 91.33.40.00

FLORALIES
PASCAL GABILLET
directeur général
9 rue des Capucins
33000 Bordeaux
                 tél. 56.22.41.84
                 télex 203 421 FLO

Steve Barnett
Sales project manager
ALBATROS
34 Harbour Rd
Aberdeen AB1 2TH

Phone (0224) 573009
Fax   (0224) 574126

● Practise spelling the names and company names as well as the addresses on the business cards.

● Practise the numbers too: there are telephone, fax and telex numbers as well as postal codes.

● Go through the same details on your own card.

● If you didn't know the names of these people, you would ask for them using their position:
e.g. *Je voudrais parler au directeur.*
Go through the cards practising this.

● Now using some of the key phrases, try asking for the various pieces of information outlined in the bubble.

coordonnées
liste des prix
coordonnées bancaires
brochure
documentation complète
catalogue

☎〰〰〰〰〰 HOW WOULD YOU SAY IN FRENCH?

1 I'm putting you through to the relevant person.
2 I'll send you a copy of our price list today.
3 Can you give me your fax number?
4 I'm very interested in the brochure your representative gave me at the Trade Fair.

Coup de fil

You are Mr or Mrs Youngson and you are ringing Monsieur Mazin, whom you met briefly last week at the Trade Fair, to ask for a copy of their price list.

CHECKING INFORMATION

PRICES

🕾〰〰〰 KEY PHRASES

I've received your company literature	J'ai bien reçu votre documentation
I've just received your catalogue	Je viens de recevoir votre catalogue
Could you tell me . . . ?	Pouvez-vous m'indiquer . . . ?
I'd like to know if . . . ?	J'aimerais savoir si . . . ?
I'd like to check . . . *I'd like to have a few more details*	J'aurais voulu vérifier . . . J'aurais aimé avoir des précisions
It is 25 francs a bottle isn't it?	C'est bien 25 francs la bouteille, n'est-ce pas?
Just a moment, let me check	Attendez, laissez-moi vérifier
Don't hesitate to contact me if you would like further information	N'hésitez pas à me contacter si vous désirez d'autres renseignements
Can you remind me of your number?	Pouvez-vous me rappeler votre numéro?
I almost forgot	J'allais oublier

DIALOGUE 1

▷ *The sales department, please.*

▶ *Can you hold? The extension's engaged.*

▷ *Yes, I'll wait.*

〰〰〰〰

▶ *Hello? I'm putting you through to Monsieur Martin, our sales manager.*

〰〰〰〰

▶ *Hello?*

▷ *Kate Anderson speaking from Fine Foods Ltd. in England. I rang you last week. **I've received all your company literature.** I'm ringing as **I'd like to have a few more details.***

▶ *Yes, go ahead.*

▷ *Your products are 100% natural, aren't they?*

▶ *Oh yes. They don't contain any additives or colouring.*

▷ Le service commercial, s'il vous plaît.

▶ Vous patientez? Le poste est occupé.

▷ Oui, je patiente.

〰〰〰〰

▶ Allô, vous êtes toujours en ligne? Je vous passe Monsieur Martin, notre directeur des ventes.

〰〰〰〰

▶ Allô?

▷ Bonjour, Monsieur. Kate Anderson à l'appareil de Fine Foods Ltd. en Angleterre.[1] Je vous ai téléphoné la semaine dernière. **J'ai bien reçu votre documentation.** Je vous appelle car **j'aurais aimé[2] avoir des précisions.**

▶ Oui, je vous écoute.

▷ Vos produits sont 100% naturels, n'est-ce pas?[3]

▶ Mais oui, Madame. Ils ne contiennent ni additifs ni colorants.

---

1. *Angleterre* is also used more loosely to mean Britain.

2. Another polite way of saying 'I would like', commonly used on the telephone. But *je voudrais* or *j'aimerais* could have equally well been used in this context.

3. Adding *bien . . .* and/or *n'est-ce pas* is a useful way of checking information: it is . . . isn't it?'.

▷ *Could you tell me* *the exact ingredients of the following products: reference A 579, E 632, G 710?*

▷ **Pouvez-vous m'indiquer** la composition exacte des produits suivants: référence A 579, E 632, G 710.

▶ *Yes, of course. I'll have to check them. Are there any other points?*

▶ Bien sûr. Il faut que je vérifie. Vous désirez d'autres renseignements?

▷ *No, that's all for the moment. You've got the details of where to send things, haven't you?*

▷ Non, non. C'est tout pour le moment. Vous avez mes coordonnées, n'est-ce pas?

▶ *Yes. I'll fax you the information.* *Could you remind me of your number.*

▶ Oui. Je vous envoie les renseignements par fax. **Pouvez-vous me rappeler votre numéro?**

▷ *It's 19 44 603 226814.*

▷ Faites le 19 44 603 22 68 14.

▶ *226814. Fine.* *Don't hesitate to contact me if you require any further information.*

▶ 22 68 14. Très bien. **N'hésitez pas à me contacter si vous désirez d'autres renseignements.**

▷ *Thank you. That's very kind of you.*

▷ Merci. C'est très aimable de votre part.[1]

▶ *You're welcome. Bye.*

▶ Je vous en prie. Au revoir, Madame.

▷ *Thank you and bye.*

▷ Au revoir, Monsieur, et merci.

---

1. Another way of thanking.

DIALOGUE 2

You're through to Les Vins du Pays d'Oc. Please wait a few moments.

Vous êtes en communication avec Les Vins du Pays d'Oc. Veuillez patienter quelques instants, s'il vous plaît.

〰〰〰〰

〰〰〰〰

▶ *Hello?*

▶ Allô?

▷ *Hello. Could I speak to Monsieur Dubourg, please?*

▷ Bonjour, Madame. Pourrais-je parler à Monsieur Dubourg, s'il vous plaît.

▶ *I'm sorry, Monsieur Dubourg isn't in his office at the moment. Oh, yes, he is. Hold on. Here he is now.*

〰〰〰〰〰

▶ *Dubourg here.*

▷ *Good afternoon. John Gregory here.*

▶ *Oh yes, you're the manager of a French restaurant in Bristol, aren't you.*

▷ *Yes, that's right. **I've just received** your wine catalogue. I'd like to check some information on the Sauternes.*

▶ *Certainly.*

▷ *Firstly, Château Gravelines 1982. What's the unit price?*

▶ ***Wait a moment. Just let me check.** 81, 82 . . . here it is. 32 francs a bottle.*

▷ *OK. And for a case of 12?*

▶ *368 francs.*

▷ *Sorry, I didn't catch that.*

▶ Ah, je suis désolée. Monsieur Dubourg n'est pas dans son bureau actuellement. Ah, si! Ne quittez pas. Le voilà.

〰〰〰〰〰

▶ Dubourg à l'appareil.

▷ Bonjour Monsieur. Ici John Gregory.

▶ Ah oui. Très bien. Vous êtes le gérant d'un restaurant français à Bristol, n'est-ce pas?

▷ Oui, en effet. **Je viens de recevoir**[1] votre catalogue de vins. **J'aurais voulu**[2] **vérifier** des renseignements sur le Sauternes.

▶ Avec plaisir.

▷ Premièrement: Château Gravelines, année 1982. Quel est le prix unitaire?

▶ **Attendez, laissez-moi vérifier.** 81, 82 . . . voilà. 32 francs la bouteille.[3]

▷ D'accord. Et la caisse de 12?

▶ 368 francs.

▷ Pardon, je n'ai pas très bien compris.

---

manager = *le gérant*
the unit cost = *le prix unitaire*

1. *venir de* + infinitive = 'to have just done something' e.g. *nous venons de vérifier* = we have just checked.

2. See note 2 on page 67.

3. Note the difference in the English: '**a** bottle.

▶ *300 . . . 60 . . . 8 and you'll have to add on 18.60% for VAT.*

▷ *No, VAT isn't payable on goods for export but **I would like to know if** the cost of transport is included.*

▶ *No, you'd have to add on 12.20% for that. Would you like any more information on the prices?*

▷ *No . . . oh yes, **I almost forgot.** Le Clos de la Corderie 1986. **It is 25 francs a bottle, isn't it?***

▶ *Yes, that's right.*

▷ *Splendid, well, thank you very much.*

▶ *You're welcome, Mr Gregory.*

▶ 300 . . . 60 . . . 8 et il faut ajouter 18,60%[1] pour la TVA.[2]

▷ Non, la TVA n'est pas applicable à l'exportation mais **j'aimerais savoir si** le prix du transport est compris.

▶ Ah, non. Là il faut ajouter 12,20%.[1] Vous désirez d'autres renseignements concernant les prix?

▷ Euh, non . . . ah oui. **J'allais oublier.** Le Clos de la Corderie, année 1986. **C'est bien 25 francs la bouteille[3], n'est-ce pas?**

▶ C'est cela.

▷ Parfait. Je vous remercie.

▶ A votre service, Monsieur Gregory.

---

add (on) = *ajouter*
the cost of transport = *le prix du transport*

1. There is a comma in percentages in French where there is a decimal point in English.

2. *TVA (Taxe à la Valeur Ajoutée)* = VAT. *TTC (Toutes Taxes Comprises)* = all taxes included, *HT (Hors Taxe)* = excluding tax

3. See note 3 on page 69.

☎〰〰〰〰 **SUGGESTED ACTIVITIES**

• Looking at the price list, read out the years and the prices.

DOMAINE   André Cousty, viticulteur, vous présente son tarif du 1ᵉʳ février. Valable jusqu'au 15 août.

GRÉSEILLE

	Tarif Cave		Tarif Expédition	
	Par bouteille	Par 12	Par bouteille	Par 12
Bordeaux Rouge 1988	17,50	210,00	21,00	252,00
Graves 1986	25,00	300,00	28,50	342,00
Saint-Emilion 1989	18,00	216,00	21,50	258,00
Bordeaux Blanc 1990	13,25	159,00	16,80	201,60
Pour offrir: Coffret en bois Domaine Greseille 1987	3 bouteilles 246	6 bouteilles 276	3 bouteilles 290	6 bouteilles 320

Domaine Gréseille 33600 Noaillan. Téléphone: 56.47.42.1
Dégustation-Vente:Tous les jours sauf le lundi

▣ • Follow them on the tape now. You'll notice two new wines have been added to the range. What are they and how much are they?

• Practise asking for the price as you would on the telephone.
e.g. *Quel est le prix de la bouteille de . . . ?*
    Et la caisse de 12?

• Now try checking some of the prices:
e.g. *C'est bien . . . francs la bouteille* (or *la caisse de 12*), *n'est-ce pas?*

☎〰〰〰〰 **HOW WOULD YOU SAY IN FRENCH?**

1 I've just received your fax.
2 I'd like to have a few more details.
3 Is VAT included?
4 Do you know where to send things to?

Coup de fil

You are Patrick or Patricia Gibb from SMB Products Ltd., and you are ringing Monsieur Paul Carmona to check some prices.

DISCUSSING DISCOUNTS
TERMS OF PAYMENT

🕾〰〰〰〰〰 KEY PHRASES

I'm the buyer	Je suis le responsable des achats
It all depends on the size of the order	Tout dépend de l'importance de la commande
We have a sliding scale of prices	Nous avons des tarifs dégressifs
I'm assuming it's possible to get a reduction	Je suppose qu'il est possible d'obtenir une réduction
If you place a sizeable order, we will offer you a 5% reduction	Si vous passez une commande importante, nous vous accorderons une remise de 5%
That's attractive	C'est intéressant
I'd like to know your terms of payment	Je voudrais connaître vos conditions de paiement
Payment in cash is due on receipt of the invoice	Le règlement est à effectuer au comptant à la réception de la facture
Payment within 30 days of receipt of the invoice	30 jours après réception de la facture
I'm going to think about it *I'll have to think about that*	Je vais réfléchir encore un peu Il faut que je réfléchisse
Could you put that in writing?	Pouvez-vous confirmer cela par écrit?

DIALOGUE 1

▶ Hello, Export department.

▷ Monsieur Cazalis, please.

▶ Oh, I'm sorry. Monsieur Cazalis is in Frankfurt on business at the moment. I'll put you through to his deputy, Madame Lescaret.

〰〰〰〰

▶ Hello, can I help you?

▷ Good morning. Alastair Ross speaking. I'm ringing from Glasgow. **I'm the buyer** for a Scottish company called Fashionway.

▶ Yes, how can I help you?

▷ Monsieur Cazalis sent me the catalogue of the new collection along with some samples which I really like.

▶ Yes, this new range has been very successful.

▷ Tell me, as regards the price, it is 53 francs a metre, isn't it?

▶ Yes, it is.

▶ Allô, oui, Export.

▷ Monsieur Cazalis, s'il vous plaît.

▶ Ah, je suis désolée. Monsieur Cazalis est actuellement en voyage d'affaires à Francfort. Je vous passe son adjoint, Madame Lescaret.

〰〰〰〰

▶ Oui, j'écoute.

▷ Bonjour, Madame. Alastair Ross à l'appareil. Je vous téléphone de Glasgow. **Je suis le responsable des achats** chez Fashionway, une entreprise écossaise.

▶ Oui, en quoi puis-je vous être utile?

▷ Monsieur Cazalis m'a fait parvenir le catalogue de la nouvelle collection ainsi que quelques échantillons qui me plaisent[1] énormément.

▶ Oui, cette nouvelle gamme a beaucoup de succès.

▷ Dites-moi, Madame, le prix, c'est bien 53 francs le mètre?

▶ Oui.

---

his deputy = *son adjoint*
How can I help you? = *En quoi puis-je vous être utile?*
some samples = *quelques échantillons*
this new range = *cette nouvelle gamme*

1. *plaire à quelqu'un* = (literally) 'to please (to) someone', e.g. *Ça vous plaît?* – 'Do you like it?' *Oui, ça me plaît* = 'I like it'.

▷ *I'm assuming it is possible to get a reduction. If I order 300 metres, for example, your price will come down, won't it?*

▷ **Je suppose qu'il est possible d'obtenir une réduction.** Si j'en[1] commande 300 mètres, par exemple, votre prix baissera,[2] n'est-ce pas?

▶ *Yes, if you place a sizeable order, we'll offer you a discount of 5%.*

▶ Oui. **Si vous passez une commande importante, nous vous accorderons une remise de 5%.**

▷ *5%. That's attractive. Can you also tell me about your terms of payment?*

▷ 5% vous avez dit. **C'est intéressant.** D'autre part, **je voudrais connaître vos conditions de paiement.**

▶ *Yes, it's quite straightforward. Payment in cash is due on receipt of the invoice.*

▶ C'est très simple. **Le règlement est à effectuer au comptant, à la réception de la facture.**

▷ *Right, that all sounds fine. I'd like to think about it before I make a decision, but thank you for your help.*

▷ Ecoutez, tout ça c'est parfait. **Je vais réfléchir encore un peu** avant de[3] prendre une décision mais je vous remercie de votre amabilité, Madame.

▶ *You're welcome.*

▶ Je vous en prie.

▷ *You are Madame . . . ?*

▷ Vous êtes Madame . . . ?

▶ *Madame Lescaret.*

▶ Madame Lescaret.

▷ *Just a moment, I'll write that down. Lescaret.* LES . . .

▷ Attendez, je note. LE . . .

▶ LESCARET.

▶ LESCARET.

▷ *Right. Fine, well, bye.*

▷ D'accord. Bon, eh bien, au revoir.

---

to order = *commander*
to come down (price) = *baisser*

1. *en* = 'of it, of them'; 'If I order 300 metres (of it)'. This is understood in English, but must appear in French.

2. *Si* . . . (present tense), . . . (future tense). The same as in English: 'If I order . . . , then it will be cheaper.'

3. *avant de* + infinitive (*prendre*) = 'before taking . . .', e.g. *avant de passer une commande* = 'before placing an order'.

DIALOGUE 2

▷ Hello, is that la Fromagerie de France?

▷ Allô, c'est bien la Fromagerie de France?

► Yes, it is.

► Oui, Monsieur.

▷ Could you put me through to the person in charge of sales, please?

▷ Pourriez-vous me passer la personne qui s'occupe des ventes, s'il vous plaît?

► For France or abroad?

► En France ou à l'étranger?

▷ Abroad.

▷ A l'étranger.

► Yes, of course. If you'd like to hold on for a moment, I'll put you through to Monsieur Laîné, who's in charge of the export department.

► Oui, certainement. Ne quittez pas, je vous passe Monsieur Laîné, responsable des exportations.

〰〰〰〰

〰〰〰〰

Hold on please. Trying to connect you.

Veuillez garder l'écoute. Nous recherchons votre correspondant.

〰〰〰〰

〰〰〰〰

► Hello.

► Allô, oui!

▷ Is that Monsieur Laîné?

▷ C'est bien Monsieur Laîné?

► Speaking. Who am I talking to?

► Lui-même. A qui ai-je l'honneur de parler?

▷ Nick Williams here. I'm the buyer for the Rapido chain of supermarkets in the south of England.

▷ Nick Williams à l'appareil. Je suis le responsable du service-achats des supermarchés Rapido dans le sud de l'Angleterre.

► And what can I do for you?

► Oui. En quoi puis-je vous être utile?

---

abroad = à l'étranger

▷ Well, we're going to be organising a French Food Week very shortly – you know, fruit, wine, cheeses, and so on, and we're very interested in your products, and particularly your camembert, Tradition Normande.

▷ Voilà: nous organisons très prochainement une semaine gastronomique française: fruits, vins, fromages, etc. Nous sommes donc très intéressés par vos produits. En particulier, votre camembert, Tradition Normande.

▶ I see you have already a very clear idea of what you're after. Do you know this particular item?

▶ Je vois que vous avez déjà une idée très précise. Vous connaissez cet article?

▷ One of your reps gave me some to taste at the Salon Agricole in Paris a fortnight ago. It's just what we're after. What are your prices?

▷ Un de vos représentants me l'a fait goûté il y a quinze jours, au Salon Agricole de Paris. C'est exactement le produit que nous recherchons. Vous le faites à combien?

▶ **It all depends on the size of the order. We have a sliding scale of prices.** Just a moment, let me check: 3F25 per item from 0 to 1000.

▶ **Tout dépend de l'importance de la commande. Nous avons des tarifs dégressifs.** Attendez, laissez-moi vérifier: 3F25 pièce de 0 à 1000.

▷ OK and if I order 2000, . . .?

▷ Oui, je comprends. Si j'en[1] commande 2000, . . .?

▶ . . . then the unit price will come down to 3F10. Over 3000, it's exactly 3F. And for more than 5000, the price is 2F80.

▶ . . . le prix unitaire passera[2] à 3F10. Plus de 3000, 3F tout rond. Au delà de 5000, le prix est de[3] 2F80.

▷ No, I think 2000 will be enough!

▷ Non, non, je crois que 2000, ça suffit!

▶ If you place the order today, we'll be able to give you a discount of . . . say . . . 2.5%.

▶ Si vous passez la commande aujourd'hui-même, nous pourrons vous accorder une remise de . . . disons . . . 2,5%.

---

very shortly = *très prochainement*
a fortnight ago = *il y a quinze jours*

1. See note 1 on page 74.

2. See note 2 on page 74.

3. *le prix est de* 2F = 'the price is 2 F'. Note the use of *de*.

▷ *No, look.* **I'll have to think about that.** *What about your terms of payment?*

▷ Non, écoutez, **il faut que je réfléchisse.**[1] Et vos conditions de paiement?

▶ *Payment? It's very simple –* **within 30 days of receipt of the invoice.**

▶ Le règlement? C'est très simple. **30 jours après réception de la facture.**

▷ *Good.* **Can you confirm all this in writing?**

▷ Très bien. **Pouvez-vous confirmer cela par écrit?**

▶ *I'll send you a fax confirming the prices I've just given you. But don't think about it too long! Our prices will be going up from 1st January.*

▶ Je vous envoie une télécopie confirmant les prix que je viens de vous donner. Mais ne réfléchissez pas trop longtemps! Nos prix vont augmenter à partir du 1er janvier.

---

as from = *à partir de*
payment = *le règlement*

1. *Il faut que . . .* followed by the subjunctive.

SUGGESTED ACTIVITIES

- First read out the prices to yourself, e.g. 6 livres 39.

- Practise giving someone the day's prices:
e.g. *le prix de la lotte* (monkfish) *aujourd'hui est de 7 livres 50 le kilo.*
Go through the other prices on the list.

- Now practise offering a discount:
e.g. *Si vous commandez une tonne de saumon, nous vous accorderons une remise de 15%.*
Make different examples from the grid.

Nos prix, aujourd'hui, sont les suivants:

	0 à 500kg	500kg à 1t −15%	1t à 3t −20%	3t à 5t −30%	+ 5t
Langoustines	£6.39	£5.76	£5.43	£4.50	£4.15
Coquilles St Jacques	£10.45	£9.41	£8.88	£8.56	
Saumon	£4.26	£3.84	£3.62	£3.49	£2.85
Lotte	£7.50	£6.75	£6.37	£6.15	

Prix par kilo, en livre Sterling. Prix rendu Rungis.

- Lastly, practise checking the different prices quoted:

e.g. *Si je commande 3 tonnes de langoustines, le prix sera bien de 5 livres 43, n'est-ce pas?*

(You can also use *passera à* instead of *sera*.)

🕾〰〰〰〰 HOW WOULD YOU SAY IN FRENCH?

1 Your buyer sent me some samples three days ago.
2 The price will come down if you place a large order.
3 A 6% discount, that's attractive.
4 I'll have to think about it before placing the order.

Coup de fil

Bernard Pradoux, one of your customers, is ringing you to find out if he can get a discount.

PLACING AN ORDER
DELIVERY ARRANGEMENTS

☎〰〰〰〰 KEY PHRASES

I'd like to order . . .	J'aimerais commander . . .
I'm planning to order . . .	J'ai l'intention de commander . . .
I need . . .	J'ai besoin de . . .
I need . . .	Il me faut . . .
When do you want them for?	Vous les voulez pour quand?
When do you need them by?	Il vous les faut pour quand?
Where would you like the goods delivered?	Où voulez-vous que la marchandise soit livrée?
I would like the goods to be delivered/sent to . . .	Je souhaiterais que la marchandise soit livrée/expédiée à . . .
I don't see any problem	Je n'y vois aucun inconvénient
I don't think that's a problem	Je ne pense pas que cela soit un problème
I'll let the transport company know	Je préviendrai le transporteur
I'll confirm the order by telex	Je vous confirme la commande par télex
Send me a telex to confirm	Vous me passez un télex de confirmation

DIALOGUE 1

▶ *Conserveries de Nérac, good afternoon.*

▷ *Good afternoon. Excuse me, but could you remind me who's in charge of the export department?*

▶ *Madame Reclus.*

▷ *That's right. Can you put me through to her, please?*

▶ *Yes, of course.*

〰〰〰〰〰

▷ *Hello, Madame Reclus?*

▶ *Speaking. Who's that?*

▷ *Mrs O'Reilly.*

▶ *Oh yes. How are you?*

▷ *Fine, thank you. I'm ringing as* **I'd like to order** *. . . em . . .* **I'm planning to order** *ten cases of Le Pays Gascon foie gras. It's still 58.75F for a 250 gram box, isn't it?*

▶ *I'm afraid not. Our prices went up on the 1st June. Le Pays Gascon is now 59.25F.*

▷ *Ah. I didn't know that. It's gone up by 50 centimes, you say?*

▶ *Yes, that's right.*

▶ Conserveries de Nérac, bonjour.

▷ Bonjour, Mademoiselle. Excusez-moi. Pourriez-vous me rappeler le nom de la personne qui dirige le service des exportations?

▶ Madame Reclus.

▷ Voilà, c'est ça. Vous pouvez me la passer, s'il vous plaît?

▶ Mais oui, bien sûr.

〰〰〰〰〰

▷ Allô, Madame Reclus?

▶ Elle-même. Qui est à l'appareil?

▷ Mrs O'Reilly.

▶ Ah oui! Comment allez-vous?

▷ Très bien, merci. Je vous appelle car **j'aimerais commander** . . . euh . . . **j'ai l'intention de commander** dix caisses de foie gras, le Pays Gascon. Le prix est toujours de 58,75F la boîte de 250g, n'est-ce pas?

▶ Ah non. Depuis le premier juin nos tarifs ont augmenté. Le Pays Gascon est passé à 59,25F.

▷ Ah! je ne savais pas. Une augmentation de 50 centimes, dites-vous?

▶ Oui, c'est cela.

▷ *That's not too bad. That makes 29,625F.*

▷ Ce n'est pas trop grave. Ça fait 29.625F.[1]

▶ *Just a moment and I'll check. Yes, you're right. Ah, but don't forget, since you're ordering more than eight cases, the unit price comes down to 57.90F.*

▶ Attendez, je vérifie. Oui, vous avez raison. Ah, mais n'oubliez pas, puisque vous commandez plus de huit caisses, le prix unitaire tombe à 57,90F.

▷ *That makes . . . 28,950F. OK. That's all right.*

▷ Ça fait donc . . . 28.950F. OK. Ça va.

▶ **When** *exactly* **do you want them for?**

▶ **Vous les voulez pour quand** exactement?

▷ *As quickly as possible. It's essential I have them by the end of the month.*

▷ Le plus rapidement possible. Il est indispensable que je les reçoive[2] avant la fin du mois.

▶ *Let's see. It's the 14th today. If you get the order in today, you'll get the goods em . . . let's see . . . next Wednesday. Yes. That would be right. Wednesday, in five days' time.*

▶ Voyons, nous sommes le 14.[3] Si vous passez la commande aujourd'hui-même, vous recevrez la marchandise euh . . . voyons . . . mercredi prochain. Oui. C'est bien ça. Mercredi, dans cinq jours.

▷ *Fine.* **I'll send a telex to confirm the order.**

▷ Parfait. **Je vous confirme la commande par télex.**

▶ *Please do. And thank you.*

▶ Oui, s'il vous plaît. Et merci de votre confiance.

▷ *Oh. One more point.* **I'd like the goods to be delivered to** *a different address. It's not in Manchester itself, but in the suburbs.*

▷ Oh, encore un détail. **Je souhaiterais que la marchandise soit**[2] **livrée à** une adresse différente. Pas à Manchester même, mais dans la banlieue.

That's not too bad = *Ce n'est pas trop grave*
you're right = *vous avez raison*
since/seeing that = *puisque*
as quickly as possible = *le plus rapidement possible*
the suburbs = *la banlieue*

1. Prices can either be written 29.625,75F or 29.625 F75. Notice the full stop where English has a comma and a comma where English has a full stop.

2. More phrases that are followed by the subjunctive.

3. *Nous sommes . . .*: how to express the date or day of the week. See page 131.

▶ *I don't see any problem. I'll let the transport company know. Don't worry. Just give me all the details in your telex and I'll see to everything.*

▷ *Thank you. That's very good of you. Bye.*

▶ *That's all right. Bye.*

▶ **Je n'y vois aucun inconvénient. Je préviendrai le transporteur.** Ne vous inquiétez pas! Donnez-moi tous les détails sur votre télex. Je m'occupe de tout.

▷ Merci. C'est très aimable de votre part. Au revoir.

▶ Je vous en prie. Au revoir.

---

in your telex = *sur votre telex*

DIALOGUE 2

▶ *Hello, can I help you?*

▷ *Good morning. Jane Davidson speaking. **I need** 12 tons of frozen chips before the end of the week.*

▶ *Yes. **I don't think that'll be a problem.** All the same I'll just check with our production department. If you could wait a moment, I'll call them on another line.*

〰〰〰

▶ *Hello, Mrs Davidson. These 12 tons, **when exactly do you need them by**?*

▷ *I need them by Friday at the latest.*

▶ Allô, j'écoute.

▷ Bonjour. Jane Davidson à l'appareil. Ecoutez, **j'ai besoin de** 12 tonnes de frites surgelées avant la fin de la semaine.

▶ Oui. **Je ne pense pas que cela soit**[1] **un problème.** Je vais quand même vérifier avec notre département production. Attendez, je les appelle sur un autre poste.

〰〰〰

▶ Allô, Madame Davidson. Les 12 tonnes, **il vous les faut**[2] **pour quand** exactement?

▷ Il me les faut[2] pour vendredi, au plus tard.

---

frozen chips = *des frites surgelées*
all the same = *quand même*

1. See note 2 on page 81.

2. *il me faut* (lit. 'it is necessary to me') 'I need' e.g. *il me **les** faut*: 'I need **them**'.

▶ *Let's see. It's Tuesday today. It's a bit tight but we'll say Friday 23rd.* **And where do you want them delivered?** *Preston, as usual?*

▶ Voyons, aujourd'hui nous sommes mardi.[1] C'est un peu court, hein! Nous disons donc vendredi 23. **Où voulez-vous que la marchandise soit[2] livrée?** Preston, comme d'habitude?

▷ *No, not this time. My client would like the goods sent to Cardiff – to the SWCS cold store.*

▷ Non, pas cette fois. Mon client souhaiterait que la marchandise soit[2] expédiée à Cardiff – aux entrepôts SWCS.

▶ *Right. I see.* **Send me a telex to confirm all this.** *In particular, don't forget to give me all the details of the delivery address.*

▶ Ah, oui. Je vois. **Vous me passez un télex de confirmation.** Surtout, n'oubliez pas de me donner tous les détails concernant l'adresse de la livraison.

▷ *Yes, of course.*

▷ Mais bien sûr.

▶ *Oh, wait a moment, SWCS. Do you remember there were problems last time with the times that cold store was open. Could you check so that the driver knows? I don't want there to be any problems this time.*

▶ Ah mais, attendez, SWCS. Vous vous rappelez, il y a eu un problème la dernière fois avec les heures d'ouverture de cet entrepôt frigorifique. Pourriez-vous vérifier pour que le chauffeur soit[2] au courant? Je ne veux pas qu'il y ait[1] de problème cette fois.

▷ *No, I understand perfectly. I'll put all the details in the telex. Thanks a lot.*

▷ Non, non je comprends parfaitement. Je vais vous préciser tous les détails sur le télex. Je vous remercie.

▶ *That's OK. Bye.*

▶ Je vous en prie. Au revoir.

---

that's a bit tight = *c'est un peu court*
as usual = *comme d'habitude*
the delivery address = *l'adresse de la livraison*
the cold store = *l'entrepôt frigorifique*
in the telex = *sur le télex*

1. See note 3 on page 81.
2. See note 2 on page 81.

☎〜〜〜〜 SUGGESTED ACTIVITIES

- Read through the telex.

- Complete the sentences with the information contained in it.

Le prix convenu est de ...... FF   L'entrepôt est ouvert ....
La référence à rappeler est ......   La commande s'élève à .... kg.
La livraison est à effectuer aux... La date de livraison est ....

- See if you can add any more.

```
91-03-27  18:25
Msg 923 Title : TELFRE

DE: AZUR FLORAL/AVIGNON
A : HARRIS FLOWERS
LE: 3 AVRIL 199.

CONFIRMATION COMMANDE
DATE  CHARGEMENT: LE 5 AVRIL        LIVRAISON: LE 6 AVRIL
EXP.:  HN - BANGOR - PAYS DE GALLES
MARCHANDISE: 1000 BOITES CARTONS X 5KG - JONQUILLES (DAFFODILS)

LIVRAISON: ENTREPOTS DOMINIQUE
           Z.I DE LA COTE D'AZUR
           84440 CABANNES
           TEL: 90.92.15.80    TS LES JOURS DE 6H A 10H30

NS PREVENIR EN CAS DE CONTRETEMPS
DOUANE EXPORT/DOUANE IMPORT: A NS PRECISER ULTERIEUREMENT
PRIX CONVENU: FF 1.50 X 5000 KG = FF 7500

FACTURATION A NS ADRESSER AVEC REF A RAPPELER IMPERATIVEMENT
30/002/05/91:      AZUR FLORAL
                   14 RUE DU SOLEIL
                   84000 AVIGNON
                   TEL: 90.88.00.00
                   TELEFAX: 90.20.35.35
                   TELEX: 21355F

MODALITES DE REGLEMENT: 60 JOURS FIN DE MOIS DATE RECEPTION FACTURE

SIN. SLTS          JACQUES CONTINI
```

☎〜〜〜〜 HOW WOULD YOU SAY IN FRENCH?

1 I need five crates before the end of the week.
2 If he confirms the order today, he'll get the goods in four days'
time.
3 I don't see any problem.
4 Give me all the details of the delivery in your telex.

Coup de fil

Listen to the tape and take part in the telephone conversation which
might have taken place before the above telex was sent.

CHECKING UP
LATE DELIVERY

☎〰〰〰〰 KEY PHRASES

I'm ringing you about . . .   Je vous appelle au sujet de . . .

We still haven't received anything   Nous n'avons toujours rien reçu
You still haven't received your order   Vous n'avez toujours pas été
livré

The goods were definitely sent off   Je vous assure que la
marchandise a été expédiée

You should have received the   Vous auriez dû recevoir la
goods . . .   marchandise . . .

He assured me that you would   Il m'a certifié que vous
receive . . .   recevriez . . .

Just a moment, let me get the file   Attendez, laissez-moi prendre le
dossier

I'll check with the transport   Je vais vérifier auprès du
company   transporteur

I'm really sorry to hear that   Je suis vraiment désolé(e)
d'apprendre cela
I'm really very sorry this has   Je regrette vivement que cela se
happened   soit produit

It's not too serious   Ce n'est pas trop grave
That's all right   Ça peut aller

Keep me informed   Tenez-moi au courant

DIALOGUE 1

▶ *Jardins de Marly, good morning.*

▷ *Madame Vassort, please.*

▶ *She's on a call. Do you want to hold?*

▷ *Yes, I'll hold.*

〰〰〰〰〰

The person you've asked to speak to is busy on a call at the moment. Please hold the line.

〰〰〰〰〰

▶ *Hello? Madame Vassort's line is still busy. Would you like her to ring you back?*

▷ *No, I'll hold on. It's important.*

〰〰〰〰〰

▶ *Hello.*

▷ *Madame Vassort?*

▶ *Speaking.*

▷ *Good morning. Peter Barker here. **I'm ringing you about** the delivery of the order I placed last week, on Thursday the 14th to be precise.*

▶ *Yes.*

▷ *Well, **we still haven't received anything.***

▶ Jardins de Marly, bonjour.

▷ Madame Vassort, s'il vous plaît.

▶ Son poste est occupé. Vous patientez?

▷ Oui, oui.

〰〰〰〰〰

La personne que vous avez demandée est actuellement en communication. Vous êtes prié de bien vouloir garder l'écoute.

〰〰〰〰〰

▶ Allô? Madame Vassort est toujours en ligne. Vous voulez qu'elle vous rappelle?

▷ Non, non. Je patiente. C'est important.

〰〰〰〰〰

▶ Allô.

▷ Madame Vassort?

▶ C'est elle-même.

▷ Bonjour, Madame. Peter Barker à l'appareil. **Je vous appelle au sujet de** la livraison de la commande que j'ai passée la semaine dernière, jeudi 14 exactement.

▶ Oui.

▷ Eh bien, **nous n'avons toujours rien reçu!**

▶ *What? **You still haven't
received your order? Just a
moment. Let me get the file.** Here*
*it is. The order was for 3 tons of peas
and 4 tons of frozen broccoli.*

▶ Comment? **Vous n'avez
toujours pas été livré! Attendez
... laissez-moi prendre le
dossier.** Voilà. Il s'agissait de 3
tonnes de petits pois et de 4
tonnes de brocolis surgelés.

▷ *Yes, that's it.*

▷ Oui, c'est bien ça.

▶ *But **the goods were definitely
sent off** the day before yesterday, on
the 18th. **You should have
received them** sometime yesterday
afternoon.*

▶ Je vous assure que la
marchandise a été expédiée[1]
avant-hier, le 18. **Vous auriez dû
la recevoir** hier, dans le courant
de l'après-midi.

▷ *Yes, that's right. According to
the telex you sent to confirm, we
should have received the 14 palets on
the 19th.*

▷ Oui, selon votre télex de
confirmation, nous aurions dû
recevoir les 14 palettes, le 19.

▶ *I'm really sorry to hear this. I
don't understand it. Listen, **I'll
check with the transport
company** and I'll ring you back as
soon as I've got any news.*

▶ **Je suis vraiment désolée
d'apprendre cela.** Je comprends
pas.[2] Ecoutez, **je vais vérifier
auprès du transporteur** et je
vous rappelle dès que j'ai des
informations.

▷ *Yes, if you would. **Keep me
informed.***

▷ Oui, s'il vous plaît. **Tenez-
moi au courant.**

---

the day before yesterday = *avant-hier*
according to = *selon*

1. See page 114 for the passive
construction.
2. *Ne* is frequently omitted in spoken
French.

DIALOGUE 2

▶ *Peter Barker, please.*

▶ *Peter Barker, please.*

▷ *Speaking.*

▷ *Speaking.*

▶ *Hello, Hélène Vassort here. I've
just had Manche Express on the
line. I spoke to Monsieur Plessis
who's the traffic manager.*

▶ Ici Hélène Vassort. Je viens
d'avoir Manche Express au bout
du fil. J'ai parlé à Monsieur
Plessis qui est le directeur de
l'exploitation.

---

on the line = *au bout du fil*
the traffic manager = *le directeur de
                    l'exploitation*

▷ I hope he gave you a good explanation.

▶ **He assured me you'd have** your goods around 11 o'clock. He promised me his driver was going straight to your factory in Coventry.

▷ Didn't he give you a reason for the delay?

▶ Oh yes. He said the lorry hadn't been able to get over on the ferry. He explained there had been a storm with winds of up to 120 km an hour with the result that all the crossings had been cancelled.

▷ Oh, well in that case. . . . But he did say that his driver would be here at the end of the morning.

▶ Yes, he did.

▷ OK then. **That's all right.**

▶ **I'm really very sorry this has happened.**

▷ Oh, it's the first time. And anyway **it's not too serious!**

▶ Well, hope to hear from you again soon.

▷ Bye.

▷ J'espère qu'il vous a donné une explication valable.

▶ **Il m'a certifié que[1] vous recevriez** votre marchandise vers 11 heures. Il m'a promis que[2] son chauffeur allait directement à votre usine de Coventry.

▷ Il ne vous a pas donné la raison de ce retard?

▶ Mais si![2] Il m'a dit que[1] son camion n'avait pas pu prendre le ferry. Il m'a expliqué que[1] la tempête avait soufflé à 120 km à l'heure et par conséquent, toutes les traversées avaient été annulées.[3]

▷ Dans ce cas! Il vous a bien dit que son chauffeur serait ici en fin de matinée.

▶ Oui, c'est cela.

▷ Bon, d'accord. **Ça peut aller.**

▶ **Je regrette vivement que cela se soit produit.**

▷ Oh c'est la première fois. Et puis **ce n'est pas trop grave!**

▶ Eh bien, à très bientôt, j'espère.

▷ Au revoir.

---

a good explanation = *une explication valable*
a factory = *une usine*
a storm = *une tempête*
a crossing = *une traversée*
at the end of the morning = *en fin de matinée*

1. In these sections Madame Vassort is telling Mr Barker what Monsieur Plessis has said to her. She is recounting what she has been told to someone else. This is called indirect speech. See page 121.

2. *Si* is used for 'yes' when answering a negative question.

3. See note 1 on page 87.

📞〰〰〰 SUGGESTED ACTIVITIES

• Read the section on indirect speech on page 121 and check on pages 114–17 if you are unsure of any of the tenses.

• In the example below the driver is giving his reason for being late and the company is then explaining this to someone else.

• Now try explaining why your driver is late with the reasons given below. Use the phrases in brackets to start off your sentence.

1 *J'aurai du retard parce que j'ai raté le ferry.*
(Il m'a expliqué qu'il . . .)
2 *Je suis en retard parce que le camion est tombé en panne.*
(Il m'a dit qu'il . . .)
3 *J'arriverai certainement en retard parce que tous les ports sont fermés.*
(Il m'a expliqué qu'il . . .)
4 *Je ne serai pas à l'heure parce qu'il y a une manifestation*
(demonstration).
(Il m'a dit qu'il . . .)

📞〰〰〰 HOW WOULD YOU SAY IN FRENCH?

1 You should have checked the address.
2 I've just rung the transport company.
3 According to the telex, the goods have not been sent off.
4 I'll ring you back if I have any news.

Coup de fil

You are ringing the Agences Lacombe in the light of a fax you've just received from them.

UNIT 14

COMPLAINING

PROBLEMS WITH DELIVERY

☎〜〜〜〜〜 KEY PHRASES

I'm sorry but I'm not altogether satisfied	Je regrette mais je ne suis pas entièrement satisfait(e)
The packing is unsatisfactory	L'emballage n'est pas satisfaisant
There must be a mistake	Il doit y avoir une erreur
How about this for a solution?	J'ai une solution à vous proposer
I won't invoice you for them	Je ne vous les facture pas
It was our mistake	C'était une erreur de notre part
I'll make sure this doesn't happen again	Je vais faire le nécessaire pour que cela ne se reproduise pas
It's the first time we haven't been completely satisfied	C'est la première fois que vous ne nous donnez pas entière satisfaction
I hope this won't happen again	J'espère que cet incident ne se renouvellera pas

DIALOGUE 1

▷ Seafish Ltd., good morning.

▶ Alan Turner, please.

▷ Just a moment, please. I'll put you through.

〰〰〰〰〰

▶ Mr Turner?

▷ Yes.

▶ Good morning, Jacques Le Tortorec speaking. I'm ringing you about the goods I've just received this morning.

▷ Yes, the 25 boxes of salmon.

▶ **I'm afraid I'm not altogether satisfied.**

▷ What's wrong?

▶ Several things. Firstly, I had ordered approximately 500 kg.

▷ Just a moment, let me write this down.

▶ Well, three of the boxes are not the size I asked for.

▷ **There must have been a mistake.**

▶ And then **the packing wasn't satisfactory.** There was practically no ice left when they arrived.

▷ Seafish Ltd., good morning.

▶ Alan Turner, s'il vous plaît.

▷ Oui, un instant, s'il vous plaît. Je vous le passe.

〰〰〰〰〰

▶ Monsieur Turner?

▷ Oui.

▶ Bonjour, Jacques Le Tortorec. Je vous appelle au sujet de la marchandise que je viens de recevoir ce matin.

▷ Oui, les 25 coffres de saumon.

▶ **Je regrette mais je ne suis pas entièrement satisfait.**

▷ Que se passe-t-il?

▶ Plusieurs choses. D'abord,[1] j'avais commandé[2] 500 kg environ.

▷ Attendez, je note.

▶ Eh bien, trois des boîtes ne correspondent pas à la taille demandée.

▷ **Il doit y avoir une erreur.**

▶ Et puis[1] **l'emballage n'est pas satisfaisant.** Il n'y avait pratiquement plus de glace à l'arrivée.

---

the size = la taille
approximately = environ

1. Note the succession of D'abord ... puis ... finalement = 'First ... then ... finally'.

2. 'I had ordered' = the pluperfect tense. See page 115.

▷ *I see. I assure you that . . .*

▷ Ah bon. Je vous assure que . . .

► *Yes, yes. Lastly, the health certificate was missing.*

► Oui, peut-être. Et finalement,[1] le certificat sanitaire manquait.

▷ *But I put it in the envelope myself, along with the three invoices.*

▷ Pourtant, je l'ai mis moi-même dans l'enveloppe avec les trois factures.

► *I'm sure it wasn't there.*

► Je suis certain qu'il n'y était pas.

▷ *Monsieur Le Tortorec, look. I'll check up on what you've just told me and I'll ring you back in half an hour.*

▷ Monsieur Le Tortorec, écoutez, je vais vérifier vos informations et je vous rappelle dans une demi-heure.

► *Right then, you do whatever you have to.* **It's the first time that we haven't been completely satisfied,** *but all the same . . .*

► Enfin, bref. Faites le nécessaire. **C'est la première fois que vous ne nous donnez pas entière satisfaction,** mais quand même . . .

---

health certificate = *le certificat sanitaire*
the invoice = *la facture*

1. See note 1 on page 91.

DIALOGUE 2

► *Hello, can I help you?*

► Oui, j'écoute.

▷ *Alan Turner speaking, Monsieur Le Tortorec.*

▷ Alan Turner, à l'appareil, Monsieur Le Tortorec.

► *Well, any news?*

► Alors, quoi de neuf?

Any news = *Quoi de neuf?*

▷ First of all, you're right. There was an error. The person in dispatch made a mistake. But **how about this for a solution:** I'll send you off today the three boxes you'd asked for.

▷ Premièrement,[1] vous avez raison. Il y a eu une erreur. La personne qui s'occupe des dégroupages s'est trompée. **J'ai une solution à vous proposer:** je vous envoie[2] aujourd'hui-même les trois boîtes que vous aviez demandées.[3]

▶ And what about the three I've got already? Hello? Hello? . . .

▶ Et les trois que j'ai déjà reçues? Allô? Allô? . . .

〰〰〰〰〰

〰〰〰〰〰

▷ Monsieur Le Tortorec?

▷ Monsieur Le Tortorec?

▶ Speaking. We were cut off.

▶ Oui. Nous avons été coupés.

▷ I don't know what happened. Anyway, what was I saying?

▷ Je ne comprends pas ce qui s'est passé. Bon, qu'est-ce que je disais?

▶ You were saying you'd send me the three boxes.

▶ Vous disiez que vous m'envoyiez[2] aujourd'hui-même les trois boîtes.

▷ That's right.

▷ En effet.

▶ And what about the three I've got already?

▶ Et les trois que j'ai déjà reçues?

▷ Just keep them. **I won't invoice you for them. The mistake was ours.**

▷ Vous les conservez. **Je ne vous les facture pas. C'était une erreur de notre part.**

▶ That's fine.

▶ Parfait.

---

to make a mistake = *se tromper*
to keep/retain = *conserver*
to invoice = *facturer*

1. Note this succession of points introduced by *premièrement . . . deuxièmement . . . troisème point* = firstly . . . secondly . . . thirdly.

2. French uses a present tense here which becomes an imperfect tense in the indirect speech. English uses a future tense which becomes a conditional.

3. See note 2 on page 91.

▷ Secondly, I've checked with the person in charge of production. He assured me that there was sufficient ice. I called the transport company and they assured me there hadn't been any problem with the transport. But **I will do whatever is necessary to make sure it doesn't happen again.**

▶ Good. At this time of year you'd need to increase the amount of ice.

▷ Yes, I think it's necessary. Thirdly, my secretary agrees with me that the health certificate was definitely in with all the documents. Perhaps it went missing on arrival.

▶ Right. I'll check with the customs clearance agent.

▷ **I do hope this won't happen again.**

▸ Yes, let's hope so.

▷ Deuxièmement[1] j'ai vérifié auprès du responsable de la production. Il m'a certifié que la glace était suffisante. J'ai appelé le transporteur – il m'a assuré qu'il n'y avait eu aucun problème au cours du transport. Mais **je vais faire le nécessaire pour que cela ne se reproduise pas.**

▶ Très bien. A cette époque de l'année, il faudrait que vous augmentiez la glace.

▷ Oui, je crois que c'est nécessaire. Troisième point.[1] Ma secrétaire m'a confirmé que le certificat sanitaire était bien avec tous les documents. Il s'est peut-être égaré à l'arrivée.

▶ Bon. Je vais vérifier auprès de l'agent en douane.

▷ **J'espère que cet incident ne se renouvellera pas.**

▶ Je l'espère aussi.

---

to go missing = s'égarer
customs clearance agent = l'agent en douane

1. See note 1 on page 93.

☎〰〰〰〰 HOW WOULD YOU SAY IN FRENCH?

1 I am not entirely satisfied with (de) the goods.
2 I've checked with the transport company.
3 All the documents have gone missing.
4 Since it was our mistake, we won't invoice you for them.

☎〰〰〰〰 SUGGESTED ACTIVITIES

• Go through the information on the international consignment note (CMR) checking that you can convey orally the information contained in it.

767217

LETTRE DE VOITURE INTERNATIONALE (CMR) **INTERNATIONAL CONSIGNMENT NOTE**

Sender (Name, Address, Country) Expéditeur (Nom, Adresse, Pays)	1 Customs Reference Status Référence désignation pour mise en douane 2
NORMCOOP FRUITS Blonville-Calvados (France)	Senders Agents Reference Référence de l'expéditeur de l'agent 3
Consignee (Name, Address, Country) Destinataire (Nom, Adresse, Pays) 4	Carrier (Name, Address, Country) Transporteur (Nom, Adresse, Pays) 5
INTERNATIONAL FRUITS Ashby-Kent- Angleterre	OUEST-TRANS
Place & date of taking over the goods (place, country, date) Lieu et date de la prise en charge des marchandises (Lieu, pays, date) 6	Successive Carriers Transporteurs successifs 7
Entrepots "Vergers normands" Caen. Le 21.9.92	

COPY 1 SENDER
COPY 2 CONSIGNEE
COPY 3 CARRIER

Approved by FTA /RHA /SITPRO UK 1981

Place designated for delivery of goods (place, country) Lieu prévu pour la livraison des marchandises (lieu, pays) 8	
	This carriage is subject, notwithstanding any clause to the contrary, to the Convention on the Contract for the International Carriage of Goods by Road (CMR) Ce transport est soumis nonobstant toute clause contraire à la Convention Relative au Contrat de Transport International de Marchandises par Route (CMR)

*NB FOR
DANGEROUS
GOODS

INDICATE
1 CORRECT
TECHNICAL
NAME (PROPER
SHIPPING
NAME)
2 HAZARD
CLASS
3 UN NUMBER
4 FLASHPOINT
(IF ANY)
IN °C

Marks & Nos, No & Kind of Packages, Description of Goods* Marques et Nos, No et nature des colis; Désignation des marchandises* 9	Gross weight (kg) 10 Poids Brut (kg)	Volume (m³) 11 Cubage (m³)
Commande n° 2557/9		
Pommes rouges 425 x 10kg	4250	
Reinettes (280) x 10kg	2800	
Golden 150 x 5 kg	750	
230 seulement *50 caisses manquent*		

Carriage Charges Prix de transport	12 Sender's Instructions for Customs, etc ... Instructions de l'Expéditeur (optional) 13	
Reservations Réserves 14	Documents attached Documents Annexés (optional) 15	
	Special agreements Conventions particulières (optional) 16	
Goods Received, Marchandises Reçues 17 *nombreuses caisses écrasées*	Signature of Carrier Signature du transporteur 18	Company completing this note Société émettrice 19
		Place and Date, Signature Lieu et date, Signature 20

730

Coup de fil

Take part in the dialogue on tape in which you are ringing
Normcoop to complain about the smashed boxes and also about the
fact that there are 50 boxes missing.

GETTING ANNOYED
INCORRECT INVOICES

📞〰〰〰〰〰 KEY PHRASES

I think there's been a mistake	Je crois qu'il y a une erreur
I've a complaint to make *... in your invoice no. ... of the ...*	J'ai une réclamation à formuler ... sur votre facture numéro ... datée du ...
Something's been missed out of the invoice	Il y a un oubli sur la facture
Have you sorted out my problem?	Vous avez réglé mon problème?
There's nothing I can do about it	Je n'y peux rien
This is incredible!	C'est incroyable!
Don't pay any attention to this invoice	Ne tenez pas compte de cette facture
We agree then	Nous sommes bien d'accord
I'll send you a credit note	Je vous envoie un avoir

DIALOGUE 1

▶ *Chocolats Belgilux.*

▷ *Hello, I'd like to speak to Madame De Bruycker.*

▶ *I'm sorry. She's on holiday at the moment. I can put you through to her assistant.*

▷ *Yes, that'll be fine.*

〰〰〰〰〰

▶ *Sales Department.*

▷ *Good morning. I'm ringing in connection with an invoice I've just received.*

▶ *What's it about, exactly?*

▷ *Well, **I think there's been a mistake.***

▶ *You'll have to speak to the invoice department about any mistakes. I'll put you back to the switchboard.*

〰〰〰〰〰

▶ *Switchboard, can I help you?*

▷ *Invoice department, please.*

▶ *Who is it that you want to speak to?*

▷ *I don't know. **I have a complaint to make** about several invoices. Just put me on to someone who can help.*

▶ Chocolats Belgilux.

▷ Allô, je voudrais parler à Madame De Bruycker.

▶ Je suis désolée, Monsieur. Elle est actuellement en congé. Je peux vous passer son assistante.

▷ Oui, volontiers.

〰〰〰〰〰

▶ Service des ventes.

▷ Bonjour, Mademoiselle. Je vous téléphone au sujet d'une facture que je viens de recevoir.

▶ C'est à quel sujet exactement?

▷ Eh bien, **je crois qu'il y a une erreur.**

▶ Pour les erreurs il faut s'adresser au service facturation. Je vous repasse le standard.

〰〰〰〰〰

▶ Standard, j'écoute.

▷ Le service facturation, s'il vous plaît.

▶ A qui voulez-vous parler exactement?

▷ Mais je ne sais pas moi. **J'ai une réclamation à formuler** au sujet de plusieurs factures. Passez-moi la personne concernée.

---

invoice department = *le service facturation*
switchboard = *le standard*

▶ *I think Madame Van Roy will be able to help you.*

▷ *Well, I hope so.*

〰〰〰〰

▶ *Hello, she's on a call. Will you hold?*

▷ *Look. I'm ringing from Great Britain. I've been waiting for five minutes already!*

▶ *I'm sorry.* **There's nothing I can do.** *Ah, she's free now.*

▷ *At last!*

〰〰〰〰

▶ *Invoice department.*

▷ *Good morning. George Simpson speaking. I've noticed there's a mistake* **in your invoice no.** 210390 *of 16th April. The unit price per box of chocolates is 120 FB not 1200 FB.*

▶ *Wait a moment . . . let me get the copy of the invoice. Let's see . . . Oh, my goodness! Yes, you're right. That's quite simply a computer error.*

▷ *Yes, I thought so.*

▶ **Don't pay any attention to that invoice.**

▶ Je pense que Madame Van Roy sera à même de vous renseigner.

▷ Je l'espère.

〰〰〰〰

▶ Allô, la ligne est occupée. Vous patientez?

▷ Ecoutez, Mademoiselle. Je vous appelle de Grande Bretagne. Je patiente déja depuis cinq minutes.[1]

▶ Je regrette Monsieur. **Je n'y peux rien.** Ah! Elle est libre maintenant.

▷ Ah enfin!

〰〰〰〰

▶ Facturation.

▷ Bonjour, Madame. George Simpson à l'appareil. J'ai remarqué une erreur **sur votre facture numéro** 210390, **datée du** 16 avril. Le prix unitaire des boîtes de chocolats était de 120 FB et non pas de 1200 FB.

▶ Attendez . . . laissez-moi prendre le double de la facture. Voyons . . . Mon Dieu! Oui! Vous avez raison. Il s'agit simplement d'une erreur d'ordinateur.

▷ Ah oui. Je pense bien!

▶ **Ne tenez pas compte de cette facture.**

---

copy of the invoice = *le double de la facture*
computer error = *une erreur d'ordinateur*

1. Compare this with the English translation 'I have been waiting for five minutes' and you'll notice that the present tense is used in French.

▷ You'll cancel it then, will you?

▶ Yes. Don't worry. I'll see to it that the mistake's sorted out. Sorry about that.

▷ Well, yes, but it's not the first time it's happened. I've also got your invoice no. 226897 in front of me and there's a mistake in that too.

▶ What's wrong this time?

▷ Well, something's been missed out. Madame De Bruycker who runs the sales department told me that if the order was larger than 18 tons, we'd get a reduction of 4.5%.

▶ I'm extremely sorry. I didn't know about that. I'll have to check with her and unfortunately she's on holiday. There's nothing I can do for the moment.

▷ But **this is incredible!**

▶ Look. I'll check and ring you back.

▷ I'll leave it to you. You can get hold of me from 3 o'clock onwards at 743262 – the code is 272.

▷ Vous l'annulez, n'est-ce pas?

▶ Oui. Ne vous inquiétez pas. Je fais le nécessaire pour que l'erreur soit[1] réparée. Excusez-nous.

▷ Oui, enfin, ce n'est pas la première fois que cela se produit. Tenez, j'ai sous les yeux la facture 226897. Là encore votre facture est incorrecte.

▶ De quoi s'agit-il cette fois?

▷ Eh bien, **il y a un oubli.** Madame De Bruycker qui dirige le service des ventes m'avait dit que si la commande était supérieure à 18 tonnes, nous bénéficierions[2] d'une réduction de 4,5%.

▶ Je regrette infiniment, Monsieur. Je n'étais pas au courant. Il faut que je vérifie auprès d'elle. Elle est malheureusement en vacances. Je ne peux rien faire pour le moment.

▷ Mais **c'est incroyable!**

▶ Ecoutez, je vais vérifier et je vous rappelle.

▷ Je compte sur vous, Madame. Vous pouvez me joindre à partir de 15 heures au numéro suivant: 74 32 62 précédé de l'indicatif 272.

---

to rectify (mistake) = réparer
wrong = incorrect(e)
to get hold of/contact = joindre

1. Pour que . . . and à condition que . . . are followed by the subjunctive.

2. Madame de Bruycker had obviously said, 'If the order is larger than 18 tons, you will get a discount'. Notice how this changes to become 'was larger' and 'would get' when what she says is reported.

DIALOGUE 2

▶ *Hello, Mr Simpson. Chocolats Belgilux here.*

▷ *Oh good. Well, **have you sorted out my problem?***

▶ *Yes, **there was an omission on the invoice.** Madame De Bruycker had given you a preferential rate. The invoice total now amounts to 17,390.55 FB instead of 18,210 FB.*

▷ ***We agree then.***

▶ ***I'll send you a credit note** today. Please accept my apologies.*

▷ *Provided it doesn't happen again!*

▶ Allô, Monsieur Simpson. Les Chocolats Belgilux à l'appareil.

▷ Ah parfait. Alors, **vous avez réglé mon problème?**

▶ En effet, **il y a un oubli sur la facture.** Madame De Bruycker vous a bien accordé un tarif préférentiel. Donc le montant total de la facture s'élève à 17.390,55 FB au lieu de 18.210 FB.

▷ **Nous sommes bien d'accord.**

▶ **Je vous envoie un avoir** aujourd'hui-même. Veuillez accepter toutes mes excuses.

▷ A condition que cela ne se reproduise plus.[1]

the invoice total = *le montant total*
to amount to = *s'élever à*

1. *Pour que* . . . and *à condition que* . . . are followed by the subjunctive.

☎〜〜〜〜 SUGGESTED ACTIVITIES

📼 ● You've discovered there's a mistake on this statement. On the tape you can take part in a telephone conversation where you have to explain what is wrong. But first:

1 practise the amounts involved, numbers and dates
2 run through the telephone conversation, making sure you can
   ask for the invoice department
   explain why you're ringing
   explain exactly what is wrong
   ask for a credit note for 800F to be sent.

● Imagine it's the other invoice that is wrong. Change the amounts and go through the dialogue again.

Correspondance:

Monsieur, Madame,

Le règlement correspondant au présent relevé n'est pas
enregistré au crédit de votre compte.
Si le paiement a été effectué pourriez vous retourner
cette carte en indiquant au dos le mode de règlement.
Dans le cas contraire, merci de la diligence avec
laquelle vous ferez parvenir son montant. Courtoisement

Expéditeur:

Commercialisation
des Produits Bretons
Z.I.d'Armor
35210 Rennes Cedex 01

Date	N° de Facture	Montant	
7.03.9	5890	FF15.624,30	24.012,75
21.03.9	6722	24.812.75	date envoi relevé
			30/03/9
			date paiement
			15/04/9

←—Acompte à déduire
TOTAL A PAYER —→ 40.438.05   39.739,05

Destinataire: **49.90.908/GB – n°client :65974 Fi**

Food Import Ltd
21 Springfield Road
Newcastle upon Tyne NE13 6DY

DOCUMENT A
RETOURNER AVEC
LE REGLEMENT   MERCI!

Objet
Relevé de Facture

📞〜〜〜〜〜 HOW WOULD YOU SAY IN FRENCH?

1 I agree. There is a mistake.
2 The invoice which you've just sent me is wrong.
3 If the order is larger than 100 kg, you'll get a 2.5% discount.
4 There's nothing we can do at the moment because Mr Kerr is on holiday.

Coup de fil

Now try taking part in the conversation.

UNIT **16**

DEMANDING PAYMENT

BANK DETAILS

☎〰〰〰 KEY PHRASES

We sent you an invoice for . . .	Nous vous avons adressé une facture qui s'élève à . . .
I note that payment has still not been received	Je constate que le règlement n'a toujours pas été enregistré
Can you tell me why?	Pourriez-vous m'expliquer pourquoi?
We will be forced to take legal action	Nous serons obligés d'entamer la procédure habituelle de recouvrement
Could you give me details of your bank account?	Pourriez-vous me préciser vos coordonnées bancaires?
I've personally seen to it that this invoice gets paid	J'ai fait personnellement le nécessaire pour que cette facture soit payée
Please accept my apologies for this delay in payment	Je vous prie d'accepter toutes mes excuses pour ce retard de paiement

DIALOGUE 1

▶ *Fleurop, can I help you?*

▷ *Extension 3590, please.*

▶ *Hold on.*

ᰥᰥᰥᰥ

▷ *Good afternoon. Floral UK here.*

▶ *Sorry?*

▷ *It's a company called Floral UK from Nottingham on the line.*

▶ *Who do you want to speak to?*

▷ *Madame Maréchal, your chief accountant.*

▶ *Ah accounts. You've been put through to personnel. I'll try and get you extension 3570.*

▷ *Thank you.*

ᰥᰥᰥᰥ

▶ *Accounts.*

▷ *At last, good afternoon. I've been trying to get hold of you for the last two days.*

▶ *Pardon?*

▷ *You are Madame Maréchal, aren't you?*

▶ Fleurop, j'écoute.

▷ Poste 35 90, s'il vous plaît.

▶ Ne quittez pas.

ᰥᰥᰥᰥ

▷ Bonjour Mademoiselle, Floral UK à l'appareil.

▶ Pardon?

▷ Société Floral UK de Nottingham.

▶ Qui demandez-vous?

▷ Madame Maréchal, chef-comptable.

▶ Ah, la comptabilité. Mais vous êtes ici au service du personnel. Je vais essayer de vous passer le poste 35 70.

▷ Merci Mademoiselle.

ᰥᰥᰥᰥ

▶ Comptabilité.

▷ Ah, enfin! Bonjour, Madame. Ça fait deux jours que j'essaie de vous joindre.[1]

▶ Comment?

▷ Vous êtes bien Madame Maréchal, n'est-ce pas?

---

head accountant = *le chef-comptable*
accounts department = *le service comptabilité*

1. This is another way of saying *j'essaie de vous joindre depuis deux jours* = 'I have been trying to get hold of you for two days'.

▶ I'm sorry. Madame Maréchal doesn't work here any more. She left the company two months ago. Can I help you?

▷ Steven Clark here. I run the accounts department at Floral UK. On the 22 January this year **we sent you an invoice** No. F.510 **for £6,540.80. I note that payment has still not been received.**

▶ January 22, did you say. That's three months ago.

▷ I've contacted Madame Maréchal twice. **Could you explain why** this invoice has still not been settled in spite of our reminder of 3 April?

▶ Look, I'm afraid the person who used to deal with all that doesn't work here any longer.

▷ That's no excuse.

▶ We are perhaps talking about a mistake on our side. **Could you give me the details of your bank account?**

▷ Yes. Midland Bank, Grosvenor Square, Nottingham. The sorting code is NN 564903 and the account number is 000261Y.

▶ Je regrette, Monsieur, Madame Maréchal ne travaille plus ici. Elle a quitté la société il y a deux mois. Puis-je vous renseigner?

▷ Steven Clark à l'appareil. Je dirige le service comptabilité chez Floral UK. Le 22 janvier dernier **nous vous avons adressé la facture no.** F.510 **qui s'élève à** 6540,80 livres sterling. **Je constate que le paiement n'a toujours pas été enregistré.**

▶ Le 22 janvier, dites-vous. Cela fait trois mois!

▷ A deux reprises j'ai contacté Mme Maréchal. **Pourriez-vous m'expliquer pourquoi** le règlement n'a toujours pas été effectué malgré la lettre de rappel du 3 avril?

▶ Ecoutez, Monsieur. La personne qui s'occupait du service ne travaille plus ici.

▷ Ce n'est pas une raison, Mademoiselle.

▶ Il s'agit peut-être d'une erreur de notre part. **Pourriez-vous me préciser vos coordonnées bancaires?**

▷ Oui. Les voici. Midland Bank, Grosvenor Square, Nottingham. Numéro de branche NN 564903 et numéro de compte 000261Y.

---

22 January this year = *le 22 janvier dernier*
twice/on two occasions = *à deux reprises*
in spite of = *malgré*
a reminder = *un lettre de rappel*
sort code = *le numéro de branche*
the account number = *le numéro de compte*

▶ ... 000261Y. Is that right?

▷ Yes. If this invoice is not settled in the course of the week, I'm afraid **we will be forced to take legal action.**

▶ Yes. I'll see to it.

▷ Yes. It's essential you do.

▶ ... 000261Y. C'est bien ça?

▷ Oui. Si nous ne recevions pas le paiement de cette facture dans le courant de la semaine, **nous serions obligés d'entamer la procédure habituelle de recouvrement.**

▶ Oui, oui, Monsieur. Je vais faire le nécessaire.

▷ Oui, Mademoiselle. Cela est indispensable.

DIALOGUE 2

▷ Floral UK, can I help you?

▶ Mr Clark, please.

▷ Yes, just hold on please.
〰〰〰

▶ Hello, Mr Clark?

▷ Speaking.

▶ Monsieur Latour, sales director at Fleurop.

▷ You must be ringing about the overdue invoice.

▶ That's right. **Please accept my apologies for the delay in payment.**

▷ I believe Madame Maréchal, your chief accountant, has left the company.

▷ Floral UK, Can I help you?

▶ Monsieur Clark, s'il vous plaît.

▷ Oui. Ne quittez pas.
〰〰〰

▶ Allô, Monsieur Clark?

▷ Lui-même.

▶ Monsieur Latour, directeur commercial de Fleurop.

▷ Je suppose que vous m'appelez au sujet de la facture impayée.

▶ C'est cela. **Je vous prie d'accepter toutes mes excuses pour ce retard de paiement.**

▷ Je crois que Madame Maréchal, votre chef-comptable, a quitté l'entreprise.

---

overdue invoice = *la facture impayée*

▶ *That's right. We have had a few problems with day-to-day matters since she left. But I've personally seen to it that this invoice gets paid today.*

▶ En effet. Depuis son départ nous avons quelques problèmes avec les affaires courantes. **J'ai fait personnellement le nécessaire** auprès de mes services **pour que cette facture soit payée** aujourd'hui-même.

▷ *Well, that's good.*

▷ Eh bien, c'est parfait.

▶ *I assure you it will not happen again. We are really very sorry.*

▶ Je vous assure que cela ne se reproduira pas. Excusez-nous encore.

▷ *That's all right. Goodbye.*

▷ Je vous en prie. Au revoir, Monsieur.

☎〰〰〰 SUGGESTED ACTIVITIES

• Read the reminder letter below.

Messieurs,

Après l'examen de votre situation par nos services comptables, il apparaît que, sauf erreur de notre part, votre solde reste débiteur des montants suivants:

Facture n° 539 du 31/01/199.   2.546,58
      n° 611   15/03/199.   321,74
      n° 797   30/04/199.   4.686,25

Total au 15/05/199.   7.554,57 frs

Soyez assez aimable d'en effectuer le règlement dès que possible par un moyen à votre convenance.
Nous vous prions d'agréer, Messieurs, nos sincères salutations.

Marie-José Mirambeau
Chef-comptable

📞〰〰〰〰 HOW WOULD YOU SAY IN FRENCH?

1 I've been trying to get hold of you for a week.
2 Our chief-accountant no longer works here.
3 I note that invoice no. 23449 for £369 has still not been paid in spite of our reminder.
4 Please accept my apologies for this delay in payment.

Coup de fil

Take part in the telephone conversation on tape with Madame Mirambeau. You are Graham or Gillian Stewart from Topex Ltd. You have to explain the mistake and ask for details of their bank account to get your overdue payments settled.

REVIEW
THANK YOU FOR CALLING

Bonjour. Ici Jacques Sellin. Nous sommes lundi 20 septembre. Je serai malheureusement absent toute la journée. Si toutefois, vous deviez me contacter de façon urgente, n'hésitez pas à le faire sur mon téléphone portable au 36 54 22 08. Je répète: 36 54 22 08. Ou laissez un message et je vous rappellerai dès mon retour. Merci.

Sally Norman à l'appareil. Je viens de recevoir votre nouveau catalogue. Je voudrais vérifier certains renseignements concernant les prix. Pourriez-vous me rappeler demain dans la matinée. Merci.

• Now you practise leaving the following messages. You'll find some suggestions as to what you could say below.

1 Give your name. You've just received the company literature but the price list is missing. Could he fax it? Your fax number is 302 789230.

2 Give your name. You would like to have a few more details concerning the terms of payment. Could he ring you back as soon as possible.

3 You're ringing in connection with the order you placed yesterday. You want to change the delivery address. You'll fax all the details.

SAMPLE MESSAGES

1 M . . . .
Je viens de recevoir votre documentation mais la liste des prix manque. Pourriez-vous me l'envoyer par fax. Le numéro est le suivant: 61 453 9078.

2 M . . . .
J'aurais aimé avoir des renseignements concernant les conditions de paiement. Pourriez-vous me rappeler le plus rapidement possible.

3 M . . . .

Je vous appelle au sujet de la commande que j'ai placée hier. Je souhaiterais changer l'adresse de livraison. Je vous envoie tous les détails par fax.

CHECKLIST

Can you now do the following:

1 Give your company details: name, address, telephone and fax numbers?

2 Give details of a bank account?

3 Check prices and ask about discounts?

4 Place an order and arrange for delivery?

5 Cope with problems concerning a late delivery?
                                   a wrong invoice?
                                   an overdue payment?

6 Show you are dissatisfied? Apologise for something that has gone wrong?

AND FINALLY

En raison des fêtes de fin d'année, nos bureaux seront fermés du 24 décembre 13h jusqu'au 2 janvier inclus. Veuillez laisser vos coordonnées et le motif de votre appel à la fin de ce message. Merci de votre appel et meilleurs voeux pour la nouvelle année.

KEY

UNIT 1

- Jean-Michel Brioux
Yves Carpentier
Patricia Vignet
Stephen Thompson

1 Qui est à l'appareil, s'il vous plaît?
2 Allô. Vous êtes toujours en ligne?
3 Pourrais-je parler à Monsieur Mercier?
4 Veuillez patienter, s'il vous plaît.
Ne quittez pas, s'il vous plaît.

UNIT 2

- Lyon 74 26 48 21
Belfast 0232 590609

1 Je rappellerai cet après-midi.
2 Il sera ici jusqu'à midi.
3 Elle peut vous rappeler demain matin.
4 C'est un faux numéro.

UNIT 3

1 Elle sera de retour vers 15 heures.
2 Il est en réunion toute la journée.
3 Pourriez-vous prendre un message?
4 Demandez-lui de me rappeler après 16 heures.

UNIT 4

- Je voudrais prendre rendez-vous
Je voudrais vous rencontrer
    lundi 29 octobre à 11 heures.
    mardi 30 octobre à midi.
    mercredi 31 octobre à 9h30.
    jeudi 1er novembre à 15h15.

- Lundi, je suis désolé, je serai à Toulouse toute la journée.
Mardi, j'ai malheureusement un déjeuner d'affaires à midi.
Mercredi, j'aurai une réunion à cette heure-là.
Mais jeudi, c'est un jour férié. Je ne travaille pas le jour de la Toussaint.

1 Elle ne peut pas vous recevoir à 14 heures.
2 Je suis très pris(e) toute la journée.
3 Il ne revient que mercredi 21 août.
Il ne sera pas de retour avant mercredi 21 août.
4 Je voudrais prendre rendez-vous avec elle avant la fin de la semaine.

UNIT 5

1 Ne prenez pas un taxi, prenez le RER.
2 Adressez-vous à la réception.
3 Il vaudrait mieux se garer sur la place.
4 Nos bureaux se trouvent au rez-de-chaussée.

UNIT 6

1 Il s'est renseigné.
2 Vous serait-il possible de me recevoir à 16 heures?
3 Elle a mis une heure et demie pour arriver à son travail.
4 Je viens d'arriver.

UNIT 7

1 J'ai l'intention de venir (me rendre) à Paris demain.
2 La réservation a été faite la semaine dernière.
3 J'ai loué une voiture pour me rendre à la Foire-Exposition.
4 Ne vous inquiétez pas. Cela ne pose aucun problème.

UNIT 9

1 Je vous passe la personne concernée.
2 Je vous fais parvenir notre liste de prix aujourd'hui-même.
Je vous envoie nos tarifs aujourd'hui.
3 Pouvez-vous me donner votre numéro de fax?
4 Je suis très intéressé(e) par la brochure que votre représentant m'a donnée à la Foire-Exposition.

UNIT 10

| • Sauternes | 1975 | 45,00 F (la bouteille) 540,00 F (la caisse de 12) |
| Entre-Deux-Mers | 1982 | 36,25 F (la bouteille) 425,00 F (la caisse de 12) |

1 Je viens de recevoir votre fax (votre télécopie).
2 J'aimerais avoir des précisions.
3 Est-ce que la TVA est comprise?
4 Vous avez mes coordonnées?

UNIT 8

Train No.	281	239	287	1289
Paris-Nord	07.47	13.48	16.39	23.19
Bruxelles-Midi	10.48	16.40	19.31	04.30

1 Il devait vous rencontrer en fin de matinée.
2 J'ai une affaire importante à régler.
3 Elle est désolée, elle est obligée d'annuler le rendez-vous.
4 Je regrette infiniment. Je ne peux pas faire autrement.

UNIT 11

1 Votre responsable des achats m'a fait parvenir quelques échantillons il y a trois jours.
2 Le prix baissera si vous passez une commande importante.
3 Une remise de 6%, c'est intéressant.
4 Il faut que je réfléchisse avant de passer la commande.

UNIT 12

1 J'ai besoin de cinq caisses avant la fin de la semaine.
Il me faut cinq caisses avant la fin de la semaine.
2 S'il confirme la commande aujourd'hui, il recevra la marchandise dans quatre jours.
3 Je ne pense pas que cela soit un problème.
4 Donnez-moi tous les détails de la livraison sur votre télex.

UNIT 13

• **1** Il m'a expliqué qu'il aurait du retard parce qu'il avait raté le ferry.
2 Il m'a dit qu'il était en retard parce que le camion était tombé en panne.
3 Il m'a expliqué qu'il arriverait certainement en retard parce que tous les ports étaient fermés.
4 Il m'a dit qu'il ne serait pas à l'heure parce qu'il y avait une manifestation.

1 Vous auriez dû vérifier l'adresse.
2 Je viens d'appeler le transporteur. Je viens de téléphoner au transporteur.
3 Selon le télex la marchandise n'a pas été expédiée.
4 Je vous rappellerai si j'ai des informations.

UNIT 14

1 Je ne suis pas entièrement satisfait(e) de la marchandise.
2 J'ai vérifié auprès du transporteur.
3 Tous les documents se sont égarés.
4 Puisque l'erreur était de notre part, nous ne vous les facturons pas.

UNIT 15

1 Je suis bien d'accord. Il y une erreur.
2 La facture que vous venez de m'envoyer est incorrecte.
3 Si la commande est supérieure à 100 kg, vous bénéficierez d'une remise de 2,5%.
4 Nous ne pouvons rien faire pour le moment parce que Mr Kerr est en vacances/congé.

UNIT 16

1 Ça fait une semaine que j'essaie de vous joindre.
J'essaie de vous joindre depuis une semaine.
2 Notre chef-comptable ne travaille plus ici.
3 Je constate que la facture no. 23449 qui s'élève à 369 livres sterling n'a toujours pas été réglée malgré notre lettre de rappel.
4 Je vous prie d'accepter toutes mes excuses pour ce retard de paiement.

GRAMMAR SUMMARY

QUESTIONS

There are three ways of forming a question in French:

1 *Est-ce-que vous pouvez venir à 15h30?*
2 *Pouvez-vous venir à 15h30?*
3 *Vous pouvez venir à 15h30?* **(by raising the voice at the end)**

You can also use these three different ways with the questions words: *quand, combien, comment, pourquoi, où.*

1 *Quand est-ce que vous pouvez venir?*
2 *Quand pouvez-vous venir?*
3 *Vous pouvez venir **quand**?*

NEGATIVES

ne . . . pas	*Elle **ne** sera **pas** ici demain.*
	She **won't** be here tomorrow.
ne . . . plus	*Il **ne** travaille **plus** ici.*
	He **no longer** works here.
ne . . . rien	*Je **n'**ai **rien** de prévu.*
	I have **nothing** planned.
ne . . . que	*Il **ne** revient **que** dimanche.*
	He **only** gets back on Sunday.
ne . . . jamais	*Nous **ne** travaillons **jamais** ce jour-là.*
	We **never** work on that day.
ne . . . pas non plus	*Cela **n'**est **pas** possible **non plus**.*
	That's **not** possible **either**.
ne . . . aucun	*Il **n'**y a **aucun** problème.*
	There's **no** problem.

PASSIVE CONSTRUCTION

How to form: *être* (in the appropriate tense) + past participle

Example: *Ma secrétaire **a réservé** une chambre.*
*Une chambre **a été reservée** par ma secrétaire.*
(Passive form)

*Ma secrétaire **a réservé** les billets.*
*Les billets **ont été réservés** par ma secrétaire.*
(Passive form)

Une chambre	est	réservée	Les billets	sont	réservés
	sera	réservée		seront	réservés
	a été	réservée		ont été	réservés
	avait été	réservée		avaient été	réservés

REGULAR VERBS

TÉLÉPHONER	RÉFLECHIR	ATTENDRE
Present Tense: stem is the infinitive minus the *-er* or *-ir* or *-re*		
je téléphone tu es il e nous ons vous ez ils ent	je réfléchis is it issons issez issent	j'attends s – ons ez ent
Imperfect Tense: stem is the *nous* form of the present minus the *-ons*		
je téléphonais tu ais il ait nous ions vous iez ils aient	je réfléchissais ais ait ions iez aient	j'attendais ais ait ions iez aient

TÉLÉPHONER	RÉFLECHIR	ATTENDRE
Perfect Tense: *avoir* or *être** in the present tense + past participle		
j' ai tu as il a téléphon**é** nous avons vous avez ils ont	j' ai tu as il a réfléch**i** nous avons vous avez ils ont	j' ai tu as il a attend**u** nous avons vous avez ils ont
Pluperfect Tense: *avoir* or *être** in the imperfect tense + past participle		
j' avais tu avais il avait téléphon**é** nous avions vous aviez ils avaient	j' avais tu avais il avait réfléch**i** nous avions vous aviez ils avaient	j' avais tu avais il avait attend**u** nous avions vous aviez ils avaient
Future Tense: stem is the infinitive, minus the final *e* for *re* verbs		
je téléphoner**ai** tu **as** il **a** nous **ons** vous **ez** ils **ont**	je réfléchir**ai** tu **as** il **a** nous **ons** vous **ez** ils **ont**	j' attendr**ai** tu **as** il **a** nous **ons** vous **ez** ils **ont**
Conditional Tense: stem is the same as the future		
je téléphoner**ais** tu **ais** il **ait** nous **ions** vous **iez** ils **aient**	je réfléchir**ais** tu **ais** il **ait** nous **ions** vous **iez** ils **aient**	j' attendr**ais** tu **ais** il **ait** nous **ions** vous **iez** ils **aient**

Aller, venir, arriver, partir, rentrer, retourner, entrer, sortir, monter, descendre, rester, tomber, naître, mourir, devenir, passer take *être* in the perfect tense.

IRREGULAR VERBS

	ÊTRE		AVOIR		ALLER	
Present (*Présent*)						
je/j'	suis		ai		vais	
tu	es		as		vas	
il	est		a		va	
nous	sommes		avons		allons	
vous	êtes		avez		allez	
ils	sont		ont		vont	
Imperfect (*Imparfait*)						
je/j'	étais		avais		allais	
tu	étais		avais		allais	
il	était		avait		allait	
nous	étions		avions		allions	
vous	étiez		aviez		alliez	
ils	étaient		avaient		allaient	
Perfect (*Passé composé*)						
je/j'	ai	été	ai	eu	suis	allé
tu	as	été	as	eu	es	allé
il	a	été	a	eu	est	allé
nous	avons	été	avons	eu	sommes	allés
vous	avez	été	avez	eu	êtes	allés
ils	ont	été	ont	eu	sont	allés
Pluperfect (*Plus-que-parfait*)						
je/j'	avais	été	avais	eu	étais	allé
tu	avais	été	avais	eu	étais	allé
il	avait	été	avait	eu	était	allé
nous	avions	été	avions	eu	étions	allés
vous	aviez	été	aviez	eu	étiez	allés
ils	avaient	été	avaient	eu	étaient	allés
Future (*Futur*)						
je/j'	serai		aurai		irai	
tu	seras		auras		iras	
il	sera		aura		ira	
nous	serons		aurons		irons	
vous	serez		aurez		irez	
ils	seront		auront		iront	
Conditional (*Conditionnel*)						
je/j'	serais		aurais		irais	
tu	serais		aurais		irais	
il	serait		aurait		irait	
nous	serions		aurions		irions	
vous	seriez		auriez		iriez	
ils	seraient		auraient		iraient	

FAIRE		VOULOIR		POUVOIR		DEVOIR	
fais		veux		peux		dois	
fais		veux		peux		dois	
fait		veut		peut		doit	
faisons		voulons		pouvons		devons	
faites		voulez		pouvez		devez	
font		veulent		peuvent		doivent	
faisais		voulais		pouvais		devais	
faisais		voulais		pouvais		devais	
faisait		voulait		pouvait		devait	
faisions		voulions		pouvions		devions	
faisiez		vouliez		pouviez		deviez	
faisaient		voulaient		pouvaient		devaient	
ai	fait	ai	voulu	ai	pu	ai	dû
as	fait	as	voulu	as	pu	as	dû
a	fait	a	voulu	a	pu	a	dû
avons	fait	avons	voulu	avons	pu	avons	dû
avez	fait	avez	voulu	avez	pu	avez	dû
ont	fait	ont	voulu	ont	pu	ont	dû
avais	fait	avais	voulu	avais	pu	avais	dû
avais	fait	avais	voulu	avais	pu	avais	dû
avait	fait	avait	voulu	avait	pu	avait	dû
avions	fait	avions	voulu	avions	pu	avions	dû
aviez	fait	aviez	voulu	aviez	pu	aviez	dû
avaient	fait	avaient	voulu	avaient	pu	avaient	dû
ferai		voudrai		pourrai		devrai	
feras		voudras		pourras		devras	
fera		voudra		pourra		devra	
ferons		voudrons		pourrons		devrons	
ferez		voudrez		pourrez		devrez	
feront		voudront		pourront		devront	
ferais		voudrais		pourrais		devrais	
ferais		voudrais		pourrais		devrais	
ferait		voudrait		pourrait		devrait	
ferions		voudrions		pourrions		devrions	
feriez		voudriez		pourriez		devriez	
feraient		voudraient		pourraient		devraient	

PRONOUNS

Pronouns take the place of nouns and can refer either to people or things.

Direct pronouns

Il rappellera Madame Martin.
He'll call Mrs Martin back.
Il la rappellera.
He'll call her back.

Indirect pronouns

Elle fera la commission à Madame Martin.
She'll give Mrs Martin the message.
Elle lui fera la commission.
She'll give her the message.

il	me te le la nous vous les	rappellera

elle	me te lui lui nous vous leur	fera la commission

In French some very common verbs are always followed by *à* and therefore they must always be followed by an indirect pronoun:

e.g. *parler à:*   *je vais lui parler*
     téléphoner à: je vais lui téléphoner
     demander à: je vais lui demander

Examples of word order

1 *Il rappellera Madame Martin plus tard.*   *Il la rappellera.*
2 *J'ai parlé au directeur.*   *Je lui ai parlé.*
3 *J'envoie le fax au représentant.*   *Je le lui envoie.*
4 *Je veux donner le télex à la secrétaire.*   *Je veux le lui donner.*
5 *Il m'a envoyé les documents.*   *Il me les a envoyés.*
6 *Je vous ai envoyé le catalogue.*   *Je vous l'ai envoyé.*
7 *Rappelez Monsieur Thomas.*   *Rappelez-le.*
8 *Demandez à Monsieur Leclerc.*   *Demandez-lui.*

REFLEXIVE VERBS

Those verbs where the infinitive is preceded by the reflexive pronoun *se* are called reflexive verbs. The pronouns change according to the subject but the verbs, if regular, follow the usual verb pattern. All reflexive verbs take *être* in the perfect tense.

se rappeler = to remember (to remind oneself)

Present tense			Perfect tense (with *être*)			
je	**me**	rappelle	je	**me**	suis	rappelé(e)
tu	**te**	rappelles	tu	**t'**	es	rappelé(e)
il	**se**	rappelle	il	**s'**	est	rappelé
elle	**se**	rappelle	elle	**s'**	est	rappelée
nous	**nous**	rappelons	nous	**nous**	sommes	rappelé(e)s
vous	**vous**	rappelez	vous	**vous**	êtes	rappelé(e)s
ils	**se**	rappellent	ils	**se**	sont	rappelés
elles	**se**	rappellent	elles	**se**	sont	rappelées

Examples

Se trouver
Nos bureaux se trouvent au rez-de-chaussée.
Our offices are on the ground floor.

Se renseigner
Je me suis renseigné(e).
I made enquiries.

Se tromper
Elle s'est trompée.
She made a mistake.

Se rendre
J'ai loué une voiture pour me rendre à Lyons.
I've hired a car to get to Lyons.

Se garer
Vous pouvez vous garer sur la place.
You can park in the square.

S'adresser
Adressez-vous à la réception.
Go and see reception.

S'inquiéter
Ne vous inquiétez pas.
Don't worry.

THE SUBJUNCTIVE

The subjunctive is a verb form which must be used after a number of set phrases and constructions, some of which are quite common. Only the present tense form of the subjunctive is dealt with here.

How to form the present tense singular and *ils/elles* forms

Take the *ils/elles* form of the present tense and remove the *-ent* at the end. This gives you the stem:
e.g. ils *réfléchiss*ent
To this stem the following ends are added: *-e, -es, -e, -ent*.

How to form the *nous* and *vous* forms

This is exactly the same as in the imperfect tense.

Réfléchir   **Present Tense Subjunctive**

je	réfléchiss	**e**
tu	réfléchiss	**es**
il	réfléchiss	**e**
elle	réfléchiss	**e**
nous	réfléchiss	**ions**
vous	réfléchiss	**iez**
ils	réfléchiss	**ent**
elles	réfléchiss	**ent**

There are only nine verbs which do not conform to this pattern: *être, avoir, faire, aller, pouvoir, vouloir, savoir, falloir* and *valoir*. The seven most common of these are listed below.

être	je sois	vous soyez
avoir	j'aie	vous ayez
faire	je fasse	vous fassiez
aller	j'aille	vous alliez
pouvoir	je puisse	vous pouviez
vouloir	je veuille	vous vouliez
savoir	je sache	vous sachiez

Constructions and set phrases followed by the subjunctive

Il faut que . . .	*Il faut que vous changiez.*
	You have to change.
Vous voulez que . . .	*Vous voulez que je prenne un message?*
	Do you want me to take a message?
Il vaut mieux que . . .	*Il vaut mieux que vous preniez un taxi.*
	It would be better for you to take a taxi.
Il est indispensable que . . .	*Il est indispensable que je sois là à 11 h.*
	It is essential that I'm there at 11.
Il est nécessaire que . . .	*Il est nécessaire que j'aille au bureau.*
	I have to go to the office.
Il est important que . . .	*Il est important que nous nous rencontrions.*
	It is important that we meet.
Je ne pense pas que . . .	*Je ne pense pas que ce soit un problème.*
	I don't think that's a problem.
. . . pour que . . .	*. . . pour que le chauffeur soit au courant.*
	. . . so that the driver knows about it.
. . . à condition que . . .	*. . . à condition que cela ne se reproduise pas.*
	. . . on condition it doesn't happen again.

INDIRECT SPEECH

When you recount what someone has said to you, you are using
what is called indirect speech. This is used a great deal in everyday
language, but the forms are very close to English so that direct
translations are usually possible.

The main point to notice about indirect speech is that the tense of
the verb changes as follows:

Present → Imperfect
Future → Conditional
Perfect → Pluperfect

Direct speech	Indirect speech
'Je vais aller à Paris.'	*Il m'a dit qu'il allait à Paris.*
'I'm going to Paris.'	He said he was going to Paris.
'J'irai à Paris.'	*Il m'a dit qu'il irait à Paris.*
I'll go to Paris.'	He said he would go to Paris.
'Je suis allé à Paris.'	*Il m'a dit qu'il était allé à Paris.*
'I went to Paris.'	He said he had gone to Paris.

TELEPHONE SITUATIONS

ANNOUNCING YOURSELF

Ici Joanna Smith	Joanna Smith here
John Smith à l'appareil	John Smith speaking
Elle-même	Speaking (woman)
Lui-même	Speaking (man)

INTRODUCING YOURSELF

Je m'appelle John Smith	My name is John Smith
Je suis John Smith de la société . . .	I'm John Smith from . . .
Je suis (directeur) chez . . .	I'm (director) at . . .
Je suis le responsable (des ventes) chez . . .	I'm in charge of (sales) at . . .

ASKING FOR SOMEONE IN PARTICULAR

Je voudrais parler à . . .	I'd like to speak to . . .
Pourriez-vous me passer . . .	Could you put me through to . . .

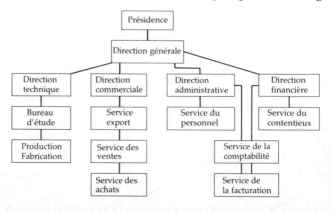

ASKING FOR THE RIGHT PERSON

Pourriez-vous me passer . . .
la personne qui dirige le (service des ventes)

Could you put me through to . . .
the person who runs the (sales) department.

le responsable du (service des ventes)

the person in charge of the (sales) department.

la personne qui s'occupe des ventes

the person who deals with sales

Pourriez-vous me rappeler le nom de la personne qui . . .

Can you remind me of the name of the person who . . .

Mme Maréchal, s'il vous plaît. Elle travaille au service de la facturation.

Mme Maréchal, please. She works in the accounts department.

Monsieur Briard, s'il vous plaît. Il travaille au service des achats.

Monsieur Briard, please. He works in the purchasing department.

Pouvez-vous me passer la personne concernée?

Can you put me through to someone who can help?

Je vous passe Monsieur 'X' qui sera à même de vous répondre/renseigner.

I'll put you through to Mr X who'll be able to help you.

DEALING WITH:

being put on hold

Ne quittez pas
Veuillez patienter }   Hold on please
Restez en ligne

an engaged line

Voulez-vous patienter?   Do you want to hold?
Oui, je patiente   Yes, I'll hold

Voulez-vous rappeler?   Do you want to ring back?
Oui, je rappellerai   Yes, I'll ring back

the person not being there

Voulez-vous qu'il vous rappelle?   Would you like him to ring you back?

Je voudrais qu'elle me rappelle   I'd like her to ring me back

Voulez-vous laisser un message?	Do you want to leave a message?
Je voudrais laisser un message	I'd like to leave a message
Pourriez-vous prendre un message?	Could you take a message?
Demandez-lui de . . .	Ask him/her to . . .
Dites-lui que . . .	Tell him/her that . . .
Je lui ferai la commission	I'll give him the message

a wrong number

C'est un faux numéro	You've got the wrong number
Vous avez fait un faux numéro	You've dialled the wrong number
Vous vous êtes trompé(e) de numéro	You made a mistake with the number
En effet. Je vous prie de m'excuser	So I have. I'm sorry to have troubled you

a bad line

La ligne est (très) mauvaise	The line is (very) bad
Il y a des grésillements sur la ligne	There are cracklings on the line
Pourriez-vous parler (un peu) plus fort?	Could you speak up (a bit)?
Vous m'entendez?	Can you hear me?
Je vous entends à peine	I can hardly hear you
Pouvez-vous me rappeler?	Can you ring me back?

being cut off

Nous avons été coupés	We were cut off.

KEEPING CONTROL OF THE SPEED AND THE SENSE

Pourriez-vous Could you *Pouvez-vous* Can you *Voulez-vous* Would you	*parler plus lentement, s'il vous plaît?* speak more slowly, please? *répéter, s'il vous plaît?* repeat that, please? *répéter plus lentement, s'il vous plaît?* repeat that more slowly, please?

G

commander . . .	I'd like to order . . .
n de commander . . .	I'm planning to order . . .
	I need . . .
. . .	I need . . .

au sujet de . . .	I'm ringing you about . . .
	I'm not . . .
satisfait(e)	. . . entirely satisfied
	. . . satisfied
ait(e)	. . . at all satisfied
n à formuler	I've a complaint to make
	There's been a mistake
	There's been an omission
as été enregistré	Payment has not been received

GS OUT

s de . . .	I'll check with . . .
otre part	It was our mistake
ir	I'll send you a credit note
iser vos	Could you give me details of
?	your bank account?

Pardon? Je n'ai pas bien compris	Sorry? I didn't catch that
Attendez, je note	Just a moment, I'll write that down
Il faut que je note	I'll have to write that down
Bien, je note	Right, I'll write that down
Attendez, je répète	Just a moment, I'll repeat that
Attendez, je vérifie	Just a moment, I'll check
Attendez, laissez-moi vérifier	Just a moment, let me check that

SHOWING YOU'RE STILL THERE

Euh . . .	Em . . .
Bon . . .	Right . . .
Eh bien . . .	Well . . .
Très bien . . .	Good . . .
C'est parfait	That's fine
En effet . . .	That's right . . .
Voyons . . .	Let's see . . .
D'accord	OK
Ah bon	I see

APOLOGISING

Je regrette . . .	I'm sorry . . .
Je suis désolé(e) . . .	I'm sorry . . .
Je suis vraiment désolé(e) . . .	I'm really sorry . . .
Je vous prie de m'excuser	I am sorry, I do apologise
Je regrette infiniment	I'm terribly sorry
Veuillez accepter toutes mes excuses	Please accept my apologies
Je regrette infiniment que cela se soit produit	I'm terribly sorry this has happened

THANKING

Merci (encore)	Thank you (once again)
Merci, c'est très gentil (de votre part)	Thank you, that's very kind (of you)
Je vous remercie, c'est très aimable (à vous)	Thank you, that's very kind (of you)

RESPONSE

Je vous en prie	That's all right
A votre service	You're welcome
Il n'y a pas de quoi	Don't mention it

OFFERING HELP

Puis-je vous renseigner?	Can I help you?
En quoi puis-je vous être utile?	How can I help you?

APPOINTMENTS

asking for an appointment

Je voudrais prendre rendez-vous avec . . .	I'd like to have an appointment with . . .
Je voudrais rencontrer . . .	I'd like to meet . . .
Monsieur Martin pourrait-il me recevoir . . .	Could Mr Martin see me . . .

offering a date

Je peux vous proposer . . .	I can offer you . . .
Je pourrais vous recevoir . . .	I could see you . . .

which is suitable

Ça tombe bien	That's OK
C'est parfait	That's fine
Ça me convient très bien	That suits me perfectly
Je n'ai rien de prévu	I've nothing arranged

which is not suitable

Ça tombe mal	That's not very suitable
Ça me paraît difficile	That's a bit difficult
Je suis déjà pris	I've already something on

confirming an appointment

Je voudrais confirmer notre rendez-vous I'd li

Nous avons bien rendez-vous à . . ., n'est-ce pas? Ou

changing an appointment

Je devais rencontrer . . .
Je vous appelle pour vous prévenir . . .
. . . qu'il me sera impossible de . . .

. . . que je ne pourrai pas . . .
. . . que je vais être obligé(e) de . .

Vous serait-il possible de . . .?

Pourriez-vous me recevoir . . .
Pourriez-vous
reculer
repousser
remettre } *le rendez-vou*
avancer

cancelling an appoint

Je suis obligé d'annuler
vous

GETTING AND CHF

Je voudrais/j'aurais vo recevoir . . .
Je voudrais avoir des sur . . .
Pourriez-vous me f
Pouvez-vous me d coordonnées?
Pourriez-vous m
J'aimerais savoir
Pourriez-vous conf écrit?

ORDERIN
Je voudrais
J'ai l'intentic
Il me faut . .
J'ai besoin de

PROBLEMS
Je vous appelle
Je ne suis pas .
. . . entièrement
. . . satisfait(e)
. . . du tout satis
J'ai une réclamat
Il y a une erreur
Il y a un oubli
Le règlement n'a p

SORTING THIN
Je vais vérifier auprè
C'est une erreur de n
Je vous envoie un av
Pourriez-vous me pré
coordonnées bancaires

QUICK REFERENCE

THE ALPHABET

(ah)	**A H K**
(é)	**B C D É G P T V W**
(eux)	**E**
(è)	**È F L M N R S Z**
(ee)	**I J X Y**
(oh)	**O**
(u)	**U Q**
as in *rue*	

FRENCH TELEPHONE ALPHABET

A	comme	Anatole	N	comme	Nicolas
B		Berthe	O		Oscar
C		Célestin	P		Pierre
D		Désiré	Q		Quintal
E		Eugène	R		René
F		François	S		Suzanne
G		Gaston	T		Thérèse
H		Henri	U		Ursule
I		Irma	V		Victor
J		Joseph	W		William
K		Kléber	X		Xavier
L		Louis	Y		Yvonne
M		Marcel	Z		Zoé

NUMBERS

0	zéro	10	dix	20	vingt
1	un	11	onze	21	vingt et un
2	deux	12	douze	22	vingt-deux
3	trois	13	treize	23	vingt-trois
4	quatre	14	quatorze	24	vingt-quatre
5	cinq	15	quinze	25	vingt-cinq
6	six	16	seize	26	vingt-six
7	sept	17	dix-sept	27	vingt-sept
8	huit	18	dix-huit	28	vingt-huit
9	neuf	19	dix-neuf	29	vingt-neuf

30	trente	100	cent
31	trente et un	200	deux cents
40	quarante	500	cinq cents
50	cinquante	1000	mille
60	soixante	5000	cinq mille
70	soixante-dix (septante)	10000	dix mille
71	soixtante et onze	100000	cent mille
80	quatre-vingts (octante)	700000	sept cent mille
81	quatre-vingt-un	1000000	un million
90	quatre-vingt-dix (nonante)		
91	quatre-vingt-onze		
99	quatre-vingt-dix-neuf		

Prices

0,45F	zéro franc quarante-cinq
1,39F	un franc trente-neuf
19,50F	dix-neuf francs cinquante
365,00F	trois cent soixante-cinq francs
1.564,29F	mille cinq cent soixante-quatre francs vingt-neuf
30.495,00F	trente mille quatre cent quatre-vingt-quinze francs
150.500,50F	cent cinquante mille cinq cent francs cinquante

Percentages

2%	deux pour cent
4,25%	quatre virgule vingt-cinq pour cent
7,50%	sept virgule cinquante pour cent
10,75%	dix virgule soixante-quinze pour cent

NOTE: **1** In French there is a comma where the decimal point comes in English
e.g. 2,5%
In French there is a full stop to separate hundreds and thousands
e.g. 124.000,55F
2 It is often easy to confuse the handwritten 1 and 7. The 7 has a tail and a bar across it, the 1 has only the tail.

7.03	n° 5890	15.624,30
21.03	n° 6722	24.812,75
	Total	40.438,05

DAYS OF THE WEEK

Monday	*lundi*		Friday	*vendredi*
Tuesday	*mardi*		Saturday	*samedi*
Wednesday	*mercredi*		Sunday	*dimanche*
Thursday	*jeudi*			

NOTE: **1** The days of the week do **not** have capital letters in French
2 On Friday = *vendredi*
On Fridays = *le vendredi*
3 Last Friday = *vendredi dernier*
Next Friday = *vendredi prochain*
4 It's Friday today = *Nous sommes vendredi aujourd'hui*

DATES

January	*janvier*	July	*juillet*
February	*février*	August	*août*
March	*mars*	September	*septembre*
April	*avril*	October	*octobre*
May	*mai*	November	*novembre*
June	*juin*	December	*décembre*

NOTE: **1** The months of the year do **not** have capital letters either
2 In January = *en janvier/au mois de janvier*
3 1st January = *le premier janvier*
19th August = *le dix-neuf août*
4 Monday, 19th August = *lundi, dix-neuf août*
5 It's the 21st today = *Nous sommes aujourd'hui le vingt et un*
6 From 21st to 24th = *du vingt et un au vingt-quatre*

Years

1992	*mil neuf cent quatre-vingt-douze*
	dix-neuf cent quatre-vingt-douze
in 1992	*en 1992*

HOLIDAYS

in France (F), Belgium (B) and Switzerland (S)

New Year's Day	(F) (B) (S)	*Le Jour de l'An*
Good Friday	(S)	*Vendredi Saint*
Easter Monday	(F) (B) (S)	*Pâques*
1st May	(F) (B) (S)	*La Fête du Travail*
8th May	(F)	*La Victoire de 1945*
Ascension Day	(F) (B) (S)	*L'Ascencion*
Whitsun	(F) (B) (S)	*La Pentecôte*
14th July	(F)	*Le Fête Nationale*
21st July	(B)	*La Fête Nationale*
1st August	(S)	*La Fête Nationale*
15th August	(F) (B) (S)	*L'Assomption*
1st November	(F) (B)	*La Toussaint*
11th November	(F) (B)	*L'Armistice de 1918*
15th November	(B)	*La Fête de la Dynastie Belge*
Christmas Day	(F) (B) (S)	*Noël*
26th December	(B) (S)	*"*

TIME

The following times are read out after the dialogues in Unit 3.

1.05 pm	13h05	treize heures cinq
2.10 pm	14h10	quatorze heures dix
3.15 pm	15h15	quinze heures quinze
4.20 pm	16h20	seize heures vingt
5.25 pm	17h25	dix-sept heures vingt-cinq
6.30 pm	18h30	dix-huit heures trente
7.35 pm	19h35	dix-neuf heures trente-cinq
8.40 pm	20h40	vingt heures quarante
9.45 pm	21h45	vingt-et-une heure quarante-cinq
10.50 pm	22h50	vingt-deux heures cinquante
11.55 pm	23h55	vingt-trois heures cinquante-cinq

at 10 o'clock = *à 10 heures*
around 10 o'clock = *vers 10 heures*
before 10 o'clock = *avant 10 heures*

after 10 o'clock = *après 10 heures*
until 10 o'clock = *jusqu'à 10 heures*
from 10 o'clock = *à partir de 10 heures*

this morning = *ce matin*
this afternoon = *cet après-midi*
this evening = *ce soir*

yesterday = *hier*
today = *aujourd'hui*
tomorrow = *demain*

in the morning = *le matin*
in the afternoon = *l'après-midi*
in the evening = *le soir*

at 8 o'clock in the morning = *à 8 heures du matin*
at 2 o'clock in the afternoon = *à 2 heures de l'après-midi*
at 11 o'clock in the evening = *à 11 heures du soir*

in the course of the morning = *dans le courant de la matinée*
at the end of the morning = *en fin de matinée*
at the beginning of the afternoon = *en début d'après-midi*
all day = *toute la journée*

a fortnight ago = *il y a quinze jours*
a week ago = *il y a une semaine*
last week = *la semaine dernière*
this week = *cette semaine*
at the beginning of the week = *au début de la semaine*
during the week = *pendant la semaine*
in the course of the week = *dans le courant de la semaine*
before the end of the week = *avant la fin de la semaine*
at the end of the week = *à la fin de la semaine*
all week = *toute la semaine/la semaine entière*
next week = *la semaine prochaine*
the week after = *la semaine suivante*
in two weeks = *en deux semaines/d'ici en deux semaines*

GLOSSARY

FRENCH – ENGLISH

absolument	*absolutely*
d'accord	*OK*
être d'accord	*to agree*
accorder	*to offer (a discount)*
actuellement	*at the moment*
s'adresser	*to go and see*
l'adjoint	*deputy*
l'affaire (f)	*matter*
affreux(se)	*terrible*
l'agence (f)	*branch (office)*
l'agenda (m)	*diary*
l'agent en douane	*customs clearance agent*
ainsi	*in this way/thus*
ajouter	*to add*
à l'angle de	*at the corner of*
annuler	*to cancel*
à l'appareil	*speaking*
appeler	*to call*
s'arrêter	*to stop*
l'ascenseur (m)	*lift*
assister à	*to attend*
attendre	*to wait*
augmenter	*to increase*
à l'avance	*in advance*
l'avoir (m)	*credit note*
avoir besoin	*to need*
de la chance	*to be lucky*
raison	*to be right*
baisser	*to come down*
la banlieue	*suburbs*
bénéficier	*to get/enjoy*
avoir besoin de	*to need*
bientôt	*soon*
blessé(e)	*hurt*
le brouillard	*fog*

le bureau d'accueil	*reception*
la cabine téléphonique	*telephone box*
la caisse	*box/crate*
le camion	*lorry*
la carte de visite	*business card*
dans ce cas	*in that case*
la catégorie	*category*
le catalogue	*catalogue*
certifier	*to assure*
le certificat	*certificate*
la chambre (simple)	*(single) room*
cher/chère	*expensive*
chercher	*to look for*
venir chercher	*to come and meet*
le chiffre	*figure*
ci-dessous	*below*
la circulation	*traffic*
le code postal	*postal code*
la commande	*order*
commander	*to order*
comment?	*sorry?*
la commission	*message*
la communication	*(phone)call*
la compagnie	*company*
complémentaire	*supplementary*
comprendre	*to understand*
le comptable	*accountant*
la comptabilité	*accounts department*
au comptant	*in cash*
compter	*to count*
concernant	*about*
les conditions de paiement	*terms of payment*
confirmer	*to confirm*

la conférence	conference
congelé(e)	deep-frozen
en congé	on holiday
connaître	to know
conserver	to keep
contacter	to contact
contenir	to contain
continuer	to continue
le contrat	contract
comme convenu	as agreed
convenir	to agree
les coordonnées (f)	details of where to contact someone
les coordonnées bancaires	bank account details
la coquille St Jacques	scallop
la correspondance	connection
le correspondant	the person being telephoned
le couloir	corridor
le coup de fil	telephone call
être au courant	to know all about something
au courant de	in the course of
croire	to believe
à côté de	beside
se débrouiller	to manage/cope
le début	beginning
la décision	decision
le dédouanement	customs clearance
dégressif	sliding
le déjeuner (d'affaires)	(business) lunch
le petit déjeuner	breakfast
déjà	already
au delà de	beyond
demander	to ask
un demi	a half
le départ	departure
dépasser	to exceed
cela dépend de	that depends on
le déplacement	business trip
depuis	since
dernier/dernière	last
dès que (possible)	as soon as (possible)
descendre	to go down
désolé(e)	sorry
deuxième	second
devoir	must; to be due to
difficile	difficult

différent	different
le directeur	director
le directeur de l'exploitation	traffic manager
diriger	to run
la documentation	company literature
quel dommage!	that's a shame!
donc	therefore
le dossier	file
le double	copy
la douche	shower
tout droit	straight ahead
à droite	to the right
l'échantillon (m)	sample
écossais	Scottish
par écrit	in writing
s'écrire	to be written/spelt
effectuer	to make (payment)
en effet	that's right
cela m'est égal	it's all the same to me
s'égarer	to go missing
s'élever à	to amount to
elle-même	speaking
l'emballage (m)	packing
l'embouteillage (m)	traffic jam
l'empêchement (m)	hitch/hold up
l'encombrement (m)	(traffic) congestion
enfin	at last
enregistrer	to record/note
entamer	to start/open
entier/entière	whole
l'entrée (f)	entrance
l'entreprise (f)	firm
l'entrepôt (m)	warehouse
l'entrepôt frigorifique	cold store
l'erreur (f)	mistake
épeler	to spell
essayer	to try
l'étage	floor
à l'étranger	abroad
expédier	to send/dispatch
l'explication (f)	explanation
l'exportation (f)	export
à l'extérieur	outside
fabriquer	to make/manufacture

en face de	opposite
facilement	easily
la facture	invoice
facturer	to invoice
faire parvenir	to send
faire le pont	to make a long weekend of it
faire le nécessaire	to do what's necessary
il faut	I, you, etc. need
il faut que ...	I, you, etc. have to ...
faux	wrong
le fax	fax
le feu rouge	traffic lights
la foire-exposition	trade-fair
formuler	to set out/formulate
plus fort	louder
frais/fraîche	fresh
français	French
les frites	chips
la gamme	range
se garer	to park
à gauche	left
gentil(le)	kind
la glace	ice
goûter	to taste
grave	bad, serious
les grésillements (m)	crackling
la grève	strike
le gérant	manager
comme d'habitude	as usual
l'heure	time
à l'heure	on time
à tout à l'heure	see you soon
les heures d'ouverture	opening times
l'horaire	time (of train)
hésiter	to hesitate
il y a	there is/... ago
l'immeuble (m)	building
impayé(e)	unpaid/outstanding
l'importance (f)	importance/size
important	important/sizeable/considerable
n'importe	it doesn't matter
l'inconvénient (m)	difficulty/snag

incroyable	unbelievable/incredible
l'indicatif (m)	telephone code
indiquer	to point out
indispensable	essential
les informations (f)	information/news
s'inquiéter	to worry
avoir l'intention de	to intend to
intéressant(e)	interesting/attractive (price)
être intéressé par	to be interested in
jamais	never
joindre	to get in touch
un jour férié	a public holiday
laisser	to leave
la langoustine	Dublin bay prawn
lentement	slowly
la lettre (de rappel)	(reminder) letter
la livraison	delivery
livrer	to deliver
lorsque	when
la lotte	monkfish
louer	to heir
lui-même	speaking
malgré	in spite of
malheureusement	unfortunately
la manifestation	demonstration
manquer	to be missing
la marchandise	the goods
mauvais(e)	bad
le message	message
mettre au point	to finalize
le mois	month
la monnaie	change
le mètre	metre
navré(e)	sorry
nécessaire	necessary
le nom de famille	surname
nouveau/nouvelle	new
le numéro	
de branche	sort code number
de compte	account number
à l'extérieur	outside number
personnel	home number
vert	freefone

obligatoire	*compulsory*	raccrocher	*to put down the*
être obligé de	*to be forced to*		*receiver*
occupé(e)	*engaged/busy*	rappeler	*to ring back/remind*
s'occuper de	*to look after/deal*	se rappeler	*to remember*
	with	rater (le train)	*to miss (the train)*
l'ordinateur (m)	*computer*	la réception	*reception*
l'oubli	*omission/oversight*	la réceptionniste	*receptionist*
		la réclamation	*complaint*
le paiement	*payment*	reculer	*to move back/put off*
paraître	*to appear*	la réduction	*reduction*
pardon?	*sorry?*	réfléchir	*to think*
un parking	*car-park*	le règlement	*settlement/payment*
de notre part	*on our behalf*	régler	*to sort out*
à partir de	*as from*	regretter	*to be sorry*
passer	*to put through*	remercier	*to thank*
se passer	*to happen*	la remise	*discount*
patienter	*to wait*	rencontrer	*to meet*
payant	*paying*	le rendez-vous	*meeting*
personnellement	*personally*	se rendre	*to go/get oneself*
à pied	*on foot*	les	*information/*
plaire à	*to like*	renseignements	*inquiries*
plusieurs	*several*	se renseigner	*to make enquiries*
faire le pont	*to make a long*	le répondeur	*answering machine*
	weekend	automatique	
le poste	*extension*	repousser	*to postpone/put back*
précis(e)	*precise*	le représentant	*representative*
préciser	*to specify/clarify*	à plusieurs	*on several occasions*
avoir des	*to have some more*	reprises	
précisions	*details*	le responsable	*person in charge*
premier/première	*first*	être en retard	*to be late*
premièrement	*firstly*	avoir du retard	*to be late*
prendre	*to take*	retardé(e)	*delayed*
prendre (un	*to catch a plane*	être de retour	*to be back*
avion)		retourner	*to go back*
près de	*near*	la réunion	*meeting*
prévenir	*to inform/warn*	revenir	*to come back*
comme prévu	*as planned*	le rez-de-chaussée	*ground-floor*
privé(e)	*private*		
pris(e)	*busy*	le saumon	*salmon*
le prix	*price*	savoir	*to know*
le problème	*problem*	la secrétaire	*secretary*
prochain(e)	*next*	le secrétariat	*secretary's office*
prochainement	*shortly*	selon	*according to*
le produit	*product*	le service	*department*
promettre	*promise*	seulement	*only*
proposer	*offer*	si	*if/yes*
puisque	*seeing that/since*	le siège	*head office*
		la société	*company/firm*
le quartier	*area*	soit . . . soit . . .	*either . . . or . . .*
quatrième	*fourth*	la sortie	*exit*
quel(le)	*which*	souhaiter	*to wish*
quinze jours	*a fortnight*	le stage	*training course*

le stand	stand (at a fair)
le standard	switchboard
la succursale	branch
le succès	success
suivant(e)	following
suivre	to follow
au sujet de	about/in connection with
supérieur(e)	higher/greater
en supplément	extra
surtout	especially
sûr(e)	sure
la taille	size
tard	late
plus tard	later
le tarif	price list/tariff/rate
la télécopie	fax
le télécopieur	fax machine
le télex	telex
tenir compte de	to take something into account
tomber en panne	to break down
tôt	early/soon
tout à coup	suddenly
tout de suite	immediately
tout droit	straight ahead
le transporteur	transport company
les travaux	roadworks
la traversée	crossing
se tromper	to make a mistake
trop	too/too much
se trouver	to be situated
la TVA	VAT
(prix) unitaire	unit (price)
l'usine (f)	factory
il vaut mieux	it is better
vérifier	to check
vers	around/about
voir	to see/go over
le vol	flight
sous les yeux	in front of me, you, etc.

ENGLISH – FRENCH

about	au sujet de/ concernant
about (approx.)	vers
abroad	à l'étranger
absolutely	absolument
according to	selon
account number	le numéro de compte
accountant	le comptable
accounts department	la comptabilité
to add	ajouter
in advance	à l'avance
ago	il y a
to agree	être d'accord/ convenir
as agreed	comme convenu
already	déjà
to amount to	s'élever à
answering machine	le répondeur automatique
to appear	paraître
area	le quartier
around (approx.)	vers
as from	à partir de
as planned	comme prévu
as soon as (possible)	dès que (possible)
to ask	demander
to assure	certifier
at last	enfin
at the moment	actuellement
to attend	assister à
attractive (price)	intéressant
to be back	être de retour
to come back	revenir
to go back	retourner
bad	grave/mauvais(e)
beginning	le début
on our behalf	de notre part
to believe	croire
beside	à côté de
it is better	il vaut mieux
beyond	au delà de
box	la caisse
branch (office)	l'agence (f)/la succursale
to break down	tomber en panne
breakfast	le petit déjeuner
building	l'immeuble (m)
business card	la carte de visite
business lunch	le déjeuner d'affaires
business trip	le déplacement
busy	pris(e)/occupé(e)

to call	appeler
to cancel	annuler
car park	un parking
in that case	dans ce cas
in cash	au comptant
to catch a plane/ train	prendre un avion/ un train
catalogue	le catalogue
category	la catégorie
certificate	le certificat
change (money)	la monnaie
to check	vérifier
chips	les frites
to clarify	préciser
cold store	l'entrepôt frigorifique
company	la compagnie/la société
company literature	la documentation
to come and meet	venir chercher
to come down	baisser
complaint	la réclamation
compulsory	obligatoire
computer	l'ordinateur (m)
to confirm	confirmer
conference	la conférence
congestion	l'encombrement (m)
connection	la correspondance
considerable	important
to contact	contacter
to contain	contenir
to continue	continuer
contract	le contrat
copy	le double
to cope	se débrouiller
corridor	le couloir
to count	compter
in the course of	au courant de
at the corner of	à l'angle de
crackling (on the line)	les grésillements (m)
crate	la caisse
credit note	l'avoir
crossing	la traversée
customs agent	l'agent en douane
customs clearance	le dédouanement
to deal with	s'occuper
decision	la décision
deep-frozen	surgelé(e)
delayed	retardé(e)

to deliver	livrer
delivery	la livraison
department	le service
departure	le départ
that depends on	cela dépend de
deputy	l'adjoint
despite	malgré
detail	le détail
to have some more details	avoir des précisions
the details of where to contact someone	les coordonnées (f)
details of one's bank account	les coordonnées bancaires
dialling code	l'indicatif (m)
diary	l'agenda (m)
different	différent
difficult	difficile
difficulty	l'inconvénient (m)
director	le directeur
discount	la remise
to dispatch	expédier
to be due to	devoir
early	tôt
easily	facilement
either . . . or	soit . . . soit
engaged	occupé(e)
to enjoy (benefit)	bénéficier
enquiries	les renseignements
to make enquiries	se renseigner
entrance	l'entrée (f)
especially	surtout
essential	indispensable
to exceed	dépasser
exit	la sortie
expensive	cher/chère
explanation	l'explication (f)
export	l'exportation (f)
extension (telephone)	le poste
extra	en supplément
factory	l'usine (f)
fax	le fax/la télécopie
fax machine	le télécopieur
figure	le chiffre
file	le dossier
to finalize	mettre au point

firm (company)	l'enterprise (f)/la société	*incredible*	incroyable
first	premier/première	*to inform*	prévenir
firstly	premièrement	*information*	les informations (f)/les
flight	le vol		renseignements (m)
floor	l'étage		
fog	le brouillard	*to have further information*	avoir des précisions
to follow	suivre		
following	suivant(e)	*injured*	blessé(e)
on foot	à pied	*to intend*	avoir l'intention de
to be forced to	obliger à		
to formulate	formuler	*to be interested in*	être intéressé(e) par
a fortnight	quinze jours		
fourth	quatrième	*invoice*	la facture
freefone	le numéro vert	*to invoice*	facturer
French	français(e)		
fresh	frais/fraîche	*kind*	gentil(le)
in front of me, you, etc.	sous les yeux	*to know*	connaître/savoir
		to know all about something	être au courant
to get (benefit)	bénéficier		
to get in touch	joindre	*last*	dernier/dernière
to get oneself (to)	se rendre (à)	*to be late*	être en retard/ avoir du retard
to go and see	s'adresser		
to go down	descendre	*later*	plus tard
to go over	voir	*to leave*	laisser
to go (to)	se rendre (à)	*(to/on the) left*	à gauche
the goods	la marchandise	*letter*	la lettre
ground-floor	le rez-de-chausée	*lift*	l'ascenseur (m)
		to like	plaire à
a half	un demi	*to look after*	s'occuper de
I, you, etc. have to . . .	il faut que . . .	*to look for*	chercher
		lorry	le camion
head office	le siège	*louder*	plus fort
to hesitate	hésiter	*to be lucky*	avoir de la chance
higher	supérieur(e)	*lunch*	le déjeuner
to hire	louer		
hitch/hold-up	l'empêchement (m)	*to make*	fabriquer
		to make (payment)	effectuer
on holiday	en congé	*to manage*	se débrouiller
home number	le numéro personnel	*manager*	le gérant
		to manufacture	fabriquer
hurt	blessé(e)	*matter*	l'affaire (f)
		it doesn't matter	n'importe
ice	la glace	*to meet*	rencontrer
if	si	*meeting*	le rendez-vous/la réunion
immediately	tout de suite		
importance	l'importance (f)	*message*	la commission/le message
important	important		
in connection with	au sujet de	*metre*	le mètre
in spite of	malgré	*to miss (the train)*	rater (le train)
to increase	augmenter	*to be missing*	manquer

to go missing	s'égarer	prawns	les langoustines (f)
mistake	l'erreur (f)	precise	précis(e)
to make a mistake	se tromper	price	le prix
monkfish	la lotte	price list	le tarif
month	le mois	private	privé(e)
to move back	reculer	problem	le problème
must	devoir	produce	le produit
		promise	promettre
near	près de	a public holiday	un jour férié
necessary	nécessaire	to put back	repousser
to do what's necessary	faire le nécessaire	to put down the receiver	raccrocher
to need	avoir besoin de	to put off	reculer
I, you, etc. need	il faut	to put through	passer
never	jamais		
new	nouveau/nouvelle	range	la gamme
news	les informations (f)	rate	le tarif
next	prochain(e)	reception	le bureau d'accueil/la réception
to note	enregistrer		
to offer (a date)	proposer	receptionist	la réceptionniste
to offer (a discount)	accorder	to record	enregistrer
OK	d'accord	reduction	la réduction
omission	l'oubli	to remember	se rappeler
on several occasions	à plusieurs reprises	to remind	rappeler
only	seulement	reminder letter	la lettre de rappel
to open	entamer	representative	le représentant
opening times	les heures d'ouverture	room	la chambre
		to be right	avoir raison
opposite	en face de	that's right	en effet
order	la commande	to the right	à droite
to order	commander	to ring back	rappeler
outside	à l'extérieur	roadworks	les travaux
outside number	le numéro à l'extérieur	to run	diriger
outstanding (payment)	impayé(e)	salmon	la saumon
		it's all the same to me	cela m'est égal
oversight	l'oubli	sample	l'échantillon (m)
packing	l'emballage (m)	scallop	la coquille St Jacques
to park	se garer	Scottish	écossais(e)
paying	payant	second	deuxième
payment	le paiement/le règlement	secretary	la secrétaire
		secretary's office	le secrétariat
person in charge	le responsable	to see	voir
personally	personnellement	see you soon	à tout à l'heure
to please	plaire à	seeing that	puisque
to point out	indiquer	to send	expédier/faire parvenir
post code	le code postal		
to postpone	reculer/repousser	serious	grave

to set out	formuler	telex	le télex
settlement	le règlement	terms of payment	les conditions de paiement
several	plusieurs		
that's a shame	quel dommage	terrible	affreux/affreuse
shortly	prochainement	to thank	remercier
shower	la douche	there is	il y a
since	depuis (time)/ puisque (as)	therefore	donc
		to think about	réfléchir
single room	la chambre simple	time	l'heure
to be situated	se trouver	on time	à l'heure
size	la taille	time (of train)	l'horaire
size (significance)	l'importance (f)	too (much)	trop
sizeable	important	trade-fair	la foire-exposition
sliding	dégressif	traffic	la circulation
slowly	lentement	traffic congestion	l'encombrement (m)
snag	l'inconvénient (m)		
soon	bientôt/tôt	traffic jam	l'embouteillage (m)
sorry	désolé(e)/navré(e)		
to be sorry	regretter	traffic lights	le feu rouge
sorry?	comment?/ pardon?	traffic manager	le directeur de l'exploitation
to sort out	régler	training course	le stage
sort code number	le numéro de branche	transport company	le transporteur
speaking	à l'appareil/ lui-même, elle-même	to try	essayer
		unbelievable	incroyable
to specify	préciser	to understand	comprendre
to spell	épeler	unfortunately	malheureusement
to be spelt	s'écrire	unit (price)	(prix) unitaire
stand (at a fair)	le stand	unpaid	impayé(e)
to start	entamer	as usual	comme d'habitude
to stop	s'arrêter		
straight ahead	tout droit	VAT	la TVA
strike	la grève		
suburbs	la banlieue	to wait	attendre/patienter
success	le succès	warehouse	l'entrepôt (m)
suddenly	tout à coup	to warn	prévenir
supplementary	complémentaire	in this way	ainsi
sure	sûr(e)	to make a long weekend	faire le pont
surname	le nom de famille		
switchboard	le standard	when	lorsque
		which	quel(le)
tariff	tarif	whole	entier/entière
to taste	goûter	to wish	souhaiter
telephone box	la cabine téléphonique	in writing	par écrit
		to be written	s'écrire
telephone call	la communication/ le coup de fil	to worry	s'inquiéter
		wrong	faux
telephone code	l'indicatif (m)		
the person being telephoned	le correspondant	yes (to negative question)	si